WORDS WORTH KNOWING

A Dictionary of Useful Words for Teenagers and Students (and everybody else...)

I0102964

Richard Nicholls

Remily Books

All enquiries should be emailed to:

Richard Nicholls
remilybooks@hotmail.co.uk

isbn : 978-0-473-23004-3

Preface

This book is intended for speakers of English, either teenagers or college and university undergraduates who need to improve their understanding of the more difficult words that appear in everyday life. This book should also be of immense use to foreign students of English who have a good command of the basics and wish to go one step further.

It is a dictionary without the thousands of plant names, minerals, chemicals, grammatical, medical, rare or, especially, the ordinary words. Declensions, colloquial words, place names, and biological and scientific words, have also mostly been left out. It comprises many words that will be familiar to the reader, but to whom the meanings are at best hazy and at worst incorrect. Where many different meanings are applicable to a word, obvious and rare or unusual definitions are not given, but those that would tax the young or inexperienced are given. The definition of '*game*', for example, is given as 'hunted wild animals', rather than the common or more infrequent uses of the word. This necessitates the partiality of the author as to the meanings included.

Each word is followed by an abbreviation indicating the class to which that word belongs. A word may belong to more than one class: for example, *flint* is an adjective and a noun.

Although a dictionary of sorts, *Words Worth Knowing* is not intended to be used in the same way as a conventional one; that is, to look up a word when one requires an accurate definition. Any good dictionary will be able to do this. The author believes that the size of this compilation lends itself to being read or browsed, not necessarily in one go but preferably with a systematic approach. Anyone learning a language will attest to the effort needed to master that language: the same is true for learning or revising words that may have been forgotten or weren't fully appreciated in the first place. The author therefore hopes that *Words Worth Knowing* will prove an ideal adjunct for the teenage student, and college or university undergraduate or reasonably advanced foreign student – and of course all those who have an interest in words and are curious about our language.

Abbreviations

abbr	-	abbreviation
acr	-	acronym
adj	-	adjective
adv	-	adverb
cf	-	compare
eg	-	for example
esp	-	especially
etc	-	et cetera
ie	-	that is
n	-	noun
pl	-	plural
pref	-	prefix
prep	-	preposition
Scand	-	Scandinavian
sg	-	singular
TM	-	trademark
US	-	United States of America
usu	-	usually
v	-	verb
/	-	used to separate definitions

A

aberration-n	an incident or way of behaving that deviates from the norm
abeyance-n	a state of postponement, esp until further facts have been obtained
abject-adj	used to emphasize that something is very bad, sad or extreme *abject poverty / a state of abject misery*
abridged-adj	shortened, with parts cut out, used of a book, play etc
abrogate-v	to officially end a law, agreement or practice
abscess-n	an accumulation of pus caused by infection or injury
abstemious-adj	frugal and restrained, esp in relation to food and drink
accede-v	to formally agree to do something
accent-n	a way of pronouncing words that is characteristic of a particular country, region or social class (*cf* **dialect**)
accord-n	an agreement, eg between nations to end hostilities
accretion-n	an increase in size by the gradual addition of new layers
Achilles heel-n	a small weakness which could expose a person or structure to harm
acolyte-n	a follower or assistant, esp someone who assists a priest in a ceremony
acoustic-adj	relating to sound and the way people hear and listen
acquiesce-v	to agree or comply with, esp by not protesting
activist-n	an active and energetic supporter of a cause
acuity-n	sharpness of vision, hearing or intellect
acumen-n	the ability to make quick decisions; shrewdness, esp in business
adenoids-n-pl	the tonsils at the back of the nose, often becoming inflamed in children
ad hoc-adj	not planned or organized in advance, but done out of necessity *The ad hoc meeting was called to discuss an important development.* (*also* **adv**)
adjutant-n	a military aide with administrative and communication duties
ad-lib-v	to say something in a play or speech that has not been planned; to improvise (*also* **adv** *and* **adj**)
admonish-v	to warn with well-intentioned sincerity
adolescence-n	the period of development between puberty and adulthood
advent-n	**1** the introduction or beginning of something *the advent of the personal computer* **2** in the Christian calendar, the four weeks before Christmas

adversary-n	an enemy or opponent
advocate-v	to recommend a course of action publicly
-n	someone who supports a cause
aegis-n	something done under the aegis of an organization is done with its support and protection
aesthetic-adj	relating to the appreciation of beauty and good taste
affectation-n	a manner of speech or behaviour that seems unnatural or insincere
affidavit-n	a written declaration made under oath
affront-n	a remark or action that offends or insults someone intentionally
agent provocateur -n	someone using a means to get a suspect to commit a crime and therefore expose himself
aggrandize-v	to make something appear more important than it really is (**self-aggrandize** - to make yourself seem very rich or important)
agrarian-adj	relating to the use and ownership of land, esp for agriculture
akimbo-adj	'arms akimbo' is a slightly aggressive stance with hands on hips and elbows sticking out (*also* **adv**)
à la carte-adj	an à la carte menu in a restaurant offers a choice of individually-priced dishes rather than a set meal (*also* **adv**) (*cf* **table d'hôte**)
alacrity-n	something done with alacrity is done eagerly and quickly
alderman-n	until 1974, a senior member of a local council elected by other councillors
alfresco-adv	if you eat alfresco, you eat outside in the open air (*also* **adj**)
algorithm-n	a series of steps, esp in a computer program, that produces a particular output or solution to a problem
Allah-n	the Islamic name for God
allege-v	to declare without proof
allegorical-adj	symbolic, esp in a religious or spiritual sense *an allegorical painting*
alms-n-pl	in the past, money or food given to the poor as charity
aloof-adj	unfriendly, distant
alopecia-n	excessive hair loss; baldness
altruism-n	unselfish concern for the good and well-being of other people
alumni-n-pl	the former students of a college or university
ambiance-n	(*also* **ambience**) the atmosphere of a place, often seen as favourable
ambidextrous-adj	able to use both hands well
ambiguity-n	the state of having more than one meaning, often confusingly
ambivalence-n	a state or feeling of uncertainty, of having two opposing attitudes to something

ambrosia-n	in Greek mythology, the food of the gods (*cf* **nectar**)
ameliorate-v	to ameliorate a situation is to improve it
amenable-adj	willing to accept an option; open-minded
amend-v	to change, improve or modify something (*cf* **emend**)
amicable-adj	friendly, agreeable
amphibious-adj	capable of living or operating on land and in water
anachronism-n	something that is out of place because it would not have existed 'in a particular period', eg television would be an anachronism in ancient Egypt
analogy-n	a pointed comparison between situations, intended to show similarities, eg a bird's wing is analogous to a man's arm
anaphylaxis-n	a severe and unusually bad reaction to a substance, esp to nuts or an insect sting
anarchy-n	a society without laws, esp when they existed previously
anastomosis-n	(*medical*) the surgical connection of two tubes, often blood vessels or parts of the intestine
anathema-n	if something is anathema to you, you hate or dislike it strongly
ancillary-adj	extra or additional but of secondary importance
androgynous-adj	having both male and female characteristics, used of a plant or animal
android-n	a robot with human appearance
angina-n	severe chest pain caused by insufficient blood flow to the heart
angst-n	feelings of anxiety, worry or dread
annals-n	the annual and historical records of an organization or society *The deal won him a place in the annals of City history.*
anodyne-adj	(*disapproving*) neutral, insipid, not likely to cause excitement
-n	a painkiller such as aspirin
anomaly-n	an unusual or irregular occurrence
antagonist-n	an opponent, eg in an argument or competition
antediluvian-adj	**1** in Christian mythology, dating from before the Biblical flood **2** out-dated or old-fashioned
anthology-n	a collection of poems, stories or songs by different writers
antipasto-n	(*pl* **antipasti**) in Italian cuisine, a starter or appetizer
antipathy-n	a strong dislike, hostility or hatred
antipodes-n	places at opposite points on the Earth (**the Antipodes** = Australia and New Zealand, often used humorously)
antiquity-n	the distant past, esp the time of the ancient Greeks, Egyptians and Romans
anti-Semitic-adj	anti-Jewish

3

Anzac-n-acr	a soldier in the Australian and New Zealand Army Corps in World War I
apartheid-n	racial segregation, esp within the former political system in South Africa
apathetic-adj	not interested or enthusiastic; indifferent
aphorism-n	a short witty phrase that expresses an insight or a general truth, eg 'if it ain't broke, don't fix it'
aplomb-n	if you do something with aplomb, you do it with ease and confidence
apocryphal-adj	an apocryphal story is widely known or believed, but may not be true
apoplectic-adj	extremely angry; red-faced with fury
appease-v	to pacify someone, esp by agreeing to their demands
apposite-adj	relevant to the topic being discussed; appropriate
appraise-v	to evaluate the worth, merit or usefulness of something or someone
aqueduct-n	a tunnel or bridge conveying water across a valley (*cf* **viaduct**)
arcadian-adj	relating to an imagined rural paradise
arcane-adj	secret or mysterious knowledge *the arcane science of alchemy*
arch-pref	highest ranking / supreme (**arch-rival** = the person who is your greatest enemy)
archipelago-n	a group of islands in a large body of water
architrave-n	the frame around a door or window
archive-n	the historical records of an organization, stored for retrieval / the place in which these are stored
ardent-adj	passionate, used esp to describe a keen supporter of someone or something
arid-adj	arid land is very dry, so few plants can grow on it
Armageddon-n	in the Bible, the final battle that will lead to the destruction of the world and the human race
armaments-n-pl	weapons and military equipment used by an army
armistice-n	a temporary cessation of fighting, esp to arrange peace talks; a truce
arraign-v	someone who is arraigned is summoned to court to answer a criminal charge
arrant-adj	used to emphasize that someone or something is very bad or extreme *The government has dismissed the claim, calling it 'arrant nonsense'*
arriviste-n	(*disapproving*) someone who has recently become powerful and successful, esp by unscrupulous means

arrogance-n	the rude, unpleasant behaviour of someone who feels they are more important than other people
artefact-n	(*also* **artifact**) an object made by a human being, esp one of historical or cultural interest
artisan-n	a skilled worker, esp one who produces a finished object
artless-adj	open, frank and sincere
ascetic-n	a person whose way of life is simple and strict, esp because of their religious beliefs (*also* **adj**)
asinine-adj	extremely silly or stupid; ridiculous
aspersions-n-pl	(*sg* **aspersion**) unkind or unfair comments said about someone
asphalt-n	a black tar-like substance used for making the surface of roads
assail-v	to attack violently with words or actions; to assault
assert-v	to state strongly that something is true, or to declare your right to something
assiduous-adj	very careful to ensure that something is done properly; meticulous
assignation-n	a secret meeting, esp with a lover, often used humorously
assuage-v	to soothe; to relieve pain, fear or grief
asunder-adv	(*literary*) if something is torn asunder, it is split into parts *The country was torn asunder by racial conflict.*
atone-v	to make amends for wrongdoings
attaché-n	a diplomat who deals with a particular subject in an embassy or military unit
attenuate-v	to reduce in strength *The intensity of the torchlight was attenuated by distance.*
attest-v	to bear witness, esp in a court of law
attorney-n	a lawyer, esp one who represents people in court
attrition-n	1 the process of gradually weakening morale or resistance 2 the gradual wearing away of a surface, eg by friction
audit-n	an official examination of the accounts of a company (*also* **v**)
augment-v	to increase in value, size or effectiveness
auspicious-adj	favourable, eg of an omen
austere-adj	plain and simple; stern or harsh in appearance and manner
autocratic-adj	1 having complete power to rule and to make decisions 2 bossy and dictatorial; expecting to be obeyed
autonomous-adj	1 independent and self-governing, used eg of a region or country 2 able to work independently and make decisions by yourself
avant-garde-adj	very modern and experimental, used mainly to describe art and artists
avarice-n	the excessive desire for wealth; greed

aversion-n	a strong feeling of dislike towards someone or something
avid-adj	very keen and enthusiastic
avuncular-adj	friendly and helpful to a younger person, as an uncle might be
awning-n	a supported canvas roof that protects against the weather, often at the entrance to a tent
awry-adv	if something goes awry, it does not happen correctly or as planned
axiom-n	a self-evident truth, eg 'you can't have your cake and eat it'

B

ballistics-n	the study of the propulsion of projectiles through the air
banal-adj	unoriginal and uninteresting, used esp of speech or written work
bane-n	distress / misery caused to someone
	Bob's younger brother was the bane of his life.
bargeboard-n	a decorated board along the gable end of a roof
bar mitzvah-n	a religious ceremony celebrating a Jewish boy's coming of age
bayou-n	a slow-moving body of water in the southern US, leading from a river or lake and often overgrown with plants
beatnik-n	one of a group of unconventional young people in the 1950s and early 1960s; someone associated with the 'Beat Generation'
beguile-v	1 if you are beguiled by something, it attracts and fascinates you
	2 to deceive by charm
bellicose-adj	aggressive; behaving in a war-like manner
belvedere-n	a building that has a good view of the surrounding area
Benelux-n-acr	**Be**lgium, the **Ne**therlands and **Lux**embourg, considered as a group
	The Benelux Economic Union was formed in 1960.
benign-adj	mild / used to describe a tumour or growth that is not malignant ie one that does not spread
bespoke-adj	customized, used esp of clothing *a bespoke tailor*
bête noire-n	someone's bête noire is the person or thing that they dislike most
bigamist-n	someone who commits the crime of marrying while they are already married
bigot-n	someone who has prejudiced and unreasonable opinions, esp about race or politics
bijou-adj	small but fashionable, esp of a residence

billabong-n	a dead-end channel flowing from the main river, used mainly in Australia
bipartisan-adj	supported by two parties *a bipartisan agreement*
bivouac-n	a simple temporary campsite
black comedy-n	comedy in which the subject matter is concerned with death or morbid matters
blasé-adj	not easily impressed, excited or worried about things; nonchalant
blithe-adj	**1** used to describe something that is done casually, with little thought *The proposal shows a blithe disregard for individual freedom.* **2** (*literary*) happy and unconcerned
blitz-n	a swift sudden military attack, esp from the air (*also* **blitzkrieg**)
boardwalk-n	(*US*) a raised wooden walkway by the harbour or sea
bodice-n	the part of a woman's dress above the waist, usually close fitting
bohemian-adj	used to describe artistic people who live in an unconventional way (*also* **n**)
bombardier-n	a member of an aircrew responsible for dropping bombs
bombastic-adj	used of language, pompous and having the intention to impress, but with little substance
bona fide-adj	genuine or real; not intended to deceive *I had to pay £60 to become a bona fide member of the club.*
bonanza-n	unexpected good luck, esp financial in nature
borax-n	a compound of boron, used in the manufacture of soap, glazes and pesticides
borscht-n	Russian or Polish beetroot soup
boudoir-n	(*dated*) a woman's private room, often a sitting or dressing room
bough-n	a large branch of a tree
bourgeoisie, the-n	a term of contempt for the middle classes, esp the capitalist class of owners and employers
bovine-adj	**1** relating to cattle **2** (*disapproving*) used to describe someone who seems slow or stupid
boycott-v	to refuse to have dealings with an organization, as a protest, in order to coerce them to do something (*also* **n**)
brachial-adj	relating to the arm
brackish-adj	briny; relating to salt water
braise-v	to cook food slowly in a covered dish with a little liquid
brawn-n	muscular strength, often contrasted with intelligence *They have the brawn, but unfortunately not the brains.*

brazen-adj	not embarrassed about behaving wrongly or immorally; audacious
brevity-n	the economical use of words in writing or speech; conciseness
briar-n	(*also* **brier**) a thorny wild plant, esp a wild rose
bridle-n	a harness around a horse's head and mouth that enables its rider to control it
brigade-n	an organisation of people brought together for a purpose, eg the fire brigade
brine-n	concentrated salt water, used esp for preserving food
brinkmanship-n	the act of taking to the edge of war, to gain an advantage
brisket-n	a cut of meat from the breast of an animal, esp beef
brogues-n-pl	**1** sturdy leather boots
	2 an accent, esp of an English-speaking Irishman
browbeat-v	to force someone into submission using intimidation
brunch-n-acr	a mid-morning meal combining both **br**eakfast and l**unch**
brut-adj	used to describe dry wine, esp sparkling wine and champagne
bucolic-adj	(*literary*) relating to the countryside and rural life
bulkhead-n	a wall or partition between sections of a ship or aircraft
bulwark-n	a natural or man-made wall used as a defence
bunion-n	a large painful lump at the first joint of the big toe
bunting-n	rows of brightly coloured flags, used to decorate streets and buildings for parades and celebrations
burka-n	a garment worn by many Muslim women in public, covering all but the wearer's eyes
burlesque-n	a humorous literary or dramatic work that mocks or satirizes
bursar-n	the financial administrator of a school, college or university

C

cabal-n	(*disapproving*) a small group of people who make secret plans, esp with political aims
cabriolet-n	a sports car with a soft, fold-down roof; a convertible
cache-n	**1** a secret store, eg of weapons, drugs or explosives
	2 an area of computer storage containing rapidly accessible data
cachet-n-sg	a certain style or quality; a mark of distinction
cadence-n	a rhythmic pattern of sound / the intonation of someone's voice
cadenza-n	an elaborate solo passage, usually near the end of a piece of music, that shows off the skill of the performer, sometimes improvised

Caesarean section-n	the procedure of delivering a baby by cutting through the mother's abdominal wall and uterus
cairn-n	a pile of stones that marks a spot, such as the top of a mountain or a boundary
cajole-v	to persuade someone to do something using praise and flattery
calibrate-v	to set a scale on a measuring instrument by reference to a known standard
callow-adj	inexperienced or immature *a callow youth*
callus-n	thickened skin, esp on the hand or sole of the foot, caused by friction
calumny-n	a false statement about someone, made with intent to harm or slander them
calypso-n	a West Indian topical song / a type of rhythmic dance
cam-n	an asymmetric roller attached to a camshaft, used in the internal combustion engine to open and close valves
camber-n	a slight curve in the surface of a road, to aid water drainage
cameo-n	**1** a brief appearance by a famous actor in a film or play *memorable British cameos* (also **adj** *a cameo appearance*) **2** a semi-precious stone carved with a raised design, esp of a head
camphor-n	a strong-smelling aromatic chemical used for medicinal purposes
campus-n	the grounds and buildings of a university or college, esp on a single site *A doctor is available on campus at all times.*
canard-n	(*literary*) a deliberate falsehood, intended to mislead
candid-adj	honest and frank, esp about unpleasant truths
cant-n	hypocritical or pretentious talk, esp about religion or morality
cantilever-n	a beam or girder fixed at one end only, used as a support (*also* **adj**) *a cantilever bridge*
capitalism-n	the economic and political system based on private ownership
capitulate-v	to surrender or give in to pressure *The union is refusing to capitulate.*
capon-n	a young male chicken, castrated and fattened for eating
caprice-n	a sudden unreasonable change of mind; a whim; fickleness *the whims and caprices of fashion*
capricious-adj	likely to change your mind unexpectedly and for no reason
capstan-n	a rotating drum used as a winch, eg for pulling in an anchor
captious-adj	tending to criticize and find fault in a trivial way
carcinogen-n	a substance or agent that can cause cancer
cardinal-adj	very important or fundamental *The cardinal rule of film making is: never work with children or animals.*
carnal-adj	relating to pleasures of a sexual nature as opposed to spiritual

carousel-n	1 a fairground roundabout, esp in the US
	2 a moving belt, esp a luggage reclaim belt at an airport
carrion-n	decaying flesh of animals, which is eaten by other animals or birds
carte blanche-n	if you are given carte blanche, you have full authority to do something
cartel-n	a group of companies that act together to increase profits by controlling prices and preventing competition
casbah-n	(*also* **kasbah**) the old part of a city in Arab countries, or its markets
caste-n	in Hindu society, one of the social classes into which someone is born
castigate-v	to criticize someone severely
cataract-n	1 a medical condition in which the lens of the eye clouds over
	2 (*literary*) a large waterfall
catechism-n	in some Christian churches, a series of questions and answers about the faith that people learn in order to join the church
catharsis-n	an emotional release; the process of removing strong emotions by expressing them in some way, eg through art
catholic-adj	1 relating to the total body of the Christian church
	2 universal and inclusive
Caucasian-adj	white or pale-skinned, used of people of particular races, esp European
caucus-n	a meeting of political party members, to choose candidates for election, esp in the US
causeway-n	an elevated road or path across wet ground or water
cauterize-v	(*medical*) to treat a wound with strong heat or a chemical in order to close it or prevent infection
cavil-v	to make trivial objections or complaints (*also* **n**)
	This is not the time to cavil at the wording of the report.
censure-n	condemnation or strong criticism (*also* **v**)
chagrin-n	annoyance or disappointment, esp at your own failure
chancellor-n	a high-ranking official, eg the official representative of a university
charlatan-n	(*disapproving*) someone who claims to have special skills, eg healing skills, that they do not actually possess
chartered-adj	used to describe a professional who is fully qualified and licensed by the state *a chartered surveyor*
chary-adj	cautious or wary about something
chattel-n	(*dated*) a piece of personal property that is movable
cheroot-n	a small cigar with both ends cut flat

chicane-n	a set of sharp bends formed by barriers on a motor racing circuit
chicanery-n	an act of deceit intended to mislead people
chilblain-n	an itchy sore on the toes or fingers, caused by cold and damp
chord-n	a group of musical notes played together to create a particular sound
churlish-adj	rude, bad-tempered or unfriendly
chutzpah-n	audacity; the confidence to behave in a brazen or impertinent manner
cinders-n-pl	small pieces of burnt wood or fuel (**cinder track** = a running track made from crushed cinders)
cipher-n	a secret code used to send messages
circuitous-adj	a circuitous route is complicated and winding rather than direct
circumspect-adj	cautious; careful to consider everything before acting
circumvent-v	to circumvent a rule or restriction is to find a way around it, esp in a clever or dishonest way
citadel-n	a stronghold or fortress built for defence
citation-n	1 a quotation from a book or speech
	2 an official commendation of merit
clad-adj	1 wearing particular clothes *leather-clad / scantily clad women*
	2 covered with a layer of something
	walls clad with stucco / snow-clad mountains
clandestine-adj	hidden or secret, often used about shady or illegal activities
clarion call-n	a strong, direct or emotional appeal for people to take action
classics, the-n-pl	the study of the history and culture of Ancient Greece and Rome
clemency-n	mercy, esp in giving someone a less severe punishment
cleric-n	a member of the clergy, eg a priest or minister
climacteric-n	a crucial period when important changes take place / the menopause
cloying-adj	to become weary of a pleasure, due to excess
	the muggy, cloying heat / cloying affection
codicil-n	an addition or amendment to a will
coeliac-adj	relating to or contained in the abdomen *Coeliac disease is a disorder of the intestines caused by a sensitivity to gluten.*
coerce-v	to force a person to do something, often using threats
cognoscenti-n-pl	connoisseurs: people with special knowledge, eg about art, food, literature etc
cohort-n	1 (*disapproving*) associates or collaborators
	2 a group of people with a common link, eg a group of schoolchildren all born in the same year

colic-n	severe stomach or abdominal pain, suffered esp by babies
collateral-n	security for a loan
-adj	**1** additional but of secondary importance; supplementary
	2 collateral damage is unintended injury or damage in war
collusion-n	secret or illegal collaboration; mutual involvement in something dishonest
colonialism-n	the occupation and rule of a strong country over a weaker one, esp for trade and profit
colt-n	**1** a young male horse
	2 (*US*) a member of a junior sports team
comely-adj	(*literary*) attractive, used of a woman
commerce-n	business involved in the buying and selling of goods and services
communism-n	a political system without classes, advocating equality and communal ownership through the state
commutable-adj	able to be changed or reduced, used esp of a reduction in a court sentence
complacent-adj	(*disapproving*) content enough not to strive for better; self-satisfied
complicity-n	involvement with other people in an illegal activity or conspiracy
compote-n	fruit stewed in syrup, eaten cold as a dessert
compunction-n	a moral scruple or guilt about doing something wrong, mainly used negatively *Employers had no compunction in ignoring the employment rights of the workforce.*
conceit-n	excessive pride in your character, abilities or achievements
concerto-n	a piece of music for one or more solo instruments and an orchestra
concubine-n	(*dated*) a woman living with a man in addition to his wife, but who is socially less important
concupiscence-n	(*formal*) strong sexual desire
condescend-v	**1** to act courteously to an inferior
	2 to do something in a way that shows you think you are too important to be doing it
condiment-n	a spice for flavouring food
condole-v	to extend sympathy towards someone (**n = condolence**)
condominium-n	a block of separately owned flats that share amenities such as a garden or swimming pool, esp in the US
confederacy-n	an alliance of groups, organizations or states
confute-v	to prove that someone or something is wrong
congenital-adj	**1** a medical condition present at birth *congenital heart disease*
	2 a congenital liar is someone who cannot stop lying
conjugal-adj	relating to marriage and the rights and duties associated with it

connive-v	to connive in something wrong means to allow it to happen, or to conspire with someone to achieve it
consanguineous -adj	related by blood
conservatism-n	political ideals against change, esp rapid change
consign-v	**1** to pass something or someone to another's care
	2 to consign somebody or something to an unpleasant situation is to put them there
	My carefully researched report was consigned to the bin.
consommé-n	clear soup made from meat or vegetables
consort-n	a partner or companion / a spouse, esp of a Sovereign
conspicuous-adj	very noticeable or obvious; prominent
conspire-v	to plan an unlawful act with someone
constrain-v	to compel someone to do something
consummate-adj	complete and accomplished *a consummate pianist*
consumption-n	(*dated*) tuberculosis
contempt-n	a feeling that something or someone deserves no respect or regard
contiguous-adj	contiguous things are adjacent or touching each other
contingency-n	something negative that could happen in the future
	The instructors were ready for any contingency.
contretemps-n	an embarrassing or awkward situation in which people disagree
convivial-adj	social, friendly, lively *the convivial atmosphere of a party*
convoke-v	to organize or bring together a meeting (= **convene**)
	Only the President can convoke Parliament.
coppice-n	a small thicket of close-growing trees (= **copse**)
corollary-n	a statement or consequence that follows directly from another
corporate governance-n	an approach to running an organisation with a view to accountability and making changes where necessary
corps-n	a group of people who work together to do a particular job or task, eg in the Civil Service the diplomatic corps
corroborate-v	to provide information and evidence to support a theory
coupé-n	a two-door car with a sloping back roof
courtesan-n	in the past, a woman who was paid for sex by rich, powerful men
coven-n	an order or company of witches, usually thirteen
covenant-n	a formal written agreement that is legally recognized
covert-adj	secret or hidden, used esp of military operations and activities
coxswain-n	someone who steers a rowing boat and gives instructions to the rowers / the helmsman of a lifeboat or other small boat
crampon-n	(*usu* **pl**) a spiked metal plate attached to a boot to help mountain climbers grip the ice

13

crass-adj	crass behaviour or speech is stupid and inconsiderate *crass insensitivity*
craven-adj	very cowardly
creole-n	a language that has developed from a pidgin to become the mother-tongue used by descendants (*cf* **pidgin**)
crepitation-n	a grating or cracking sound, made eg by the ends of a broken bone
crux-n	the vital or central part, eg of a problem *the crux of the matter*
cubital-adj	(*medical*) relating to the elbow
cuckold-n	a man whose wife is having an affair, causing him to be ridiculed
cudgel-n	a heavy stick used to beat someone (*also* **v**)
culottes-n-pl	knee-length women's trousers that are cut to look like a skirt
culpable-adj	blameworthy / (*legal*) used of an action that is considered criminal *culpable negligence*
curate-n	in the Anglican church, a clergyman who assists a priest
curfew-n	a law requiring people to remain indoors after a certain time of night, usually in a war or emergency
cursory-adj	done without much thought or attention to detail; careless *a cursory glance*
cynical-adj	believing the worst of others, ie that people act out of self-interest

D

dales-n-pl	a series of valleys, used esp in names *the Yorkshire Dales*
dampcourse-n	a layer of plastic material built into a brick wall near ground level, to prevent rising damp
dank-adj	unpleasantly damp and cold, used esp of a room or cellar
darn-v	to mend a hole in a garment using long criss-crossing stitches to fill the hole
dashboard-n	the front control panel in a car, boat or light aircraft
database-n	a large collection of data stored on computer and organized for easy retrieval
daunting-adj	a daunting task, prospect or challenge is worrying and frightening
davit-n	a crane for lowering equipment into a boat or a boat into the water
Davy Jones' locker-n	the bottom of the sea, used to refer to the final resting place of drowned sailors or sunken ships

deacon-n	an ordained member of the clergy, just below the rank of priest
dean-n	**1** a senior official at a college or university
	2 a senior priest in an Anglican cathedral or large church
debacle-n	a sudden collapse or defeat
debauchery-n	immoral behaviour, esp involving sex or drugs
debonair-adj	(*dated*) elegant, well-dressed and confident, used of a man
debrief-v	to question someone after an important task, military operation or unusual experience, in order to gain information
debunk-v	to show that an idea, belief or theory is false or silly
debutante-n	a young upper-class woman who is being introduced into fashionable society
deceit-n	dishonest behaviour intended to trick or mislead people
deciduous-adj	deciduous trees lose their leaves each autumn (*cf* **evergreen**)
decimate-v	to kill large numbers, originally used to mean 'to destroy one tenth of something'
declivity-n	a downward slope
décolletage-n-sg	the front of a woman's neck and shoulders / a woman's garment with a low-cut neckline
decommission-v	to break up or withdraw something from service
	The paramilitaries must decommission their weapons.
decorum-n	correct, polite, respectful behaviour
decry-v	to criticize something openly
de facto-adj	acting or existing in fact, whether or not legally sanctioned
	His deputy has been de facto leader for the past five years.
	(*also* **adv**)
defamation-n	the damaging of someone's character or reputation by making false statements about them
deferential-adj	polite and respectful
defoliation-n	the destruction of the leaves of plants and trees, often in large forest areas, eg as a result of pollution
degradable-adj	able to undergo biological or chemical decomposition (**bio -degradable** = able to decay naturally without causing pollution)
dehiscent-adj	the spontaneous opening of a plant structure, eg a seed pod that explodes at maturity to release its contents
deign-v	(*disapproving or humorous*) to do something unwillingly or grudgingly, because you think it is beneath you
	When he deigned to speak to me at all, he was cold and distant.
deleterious-adj	(*formal*) damaging or harmful
deliverance-n	the process of being rescued from evil or danger

delude-v	to make someone, esp yourself, believe something that is not true
	We deluded ourselves into thinking we could solve the problem.
democracy-n	the system of government in which people choose their government or representatives by voting in free elections
demur-v	to express doubt or objections to a plan or idea
demure-adj	(*dated*) modest or prim, used of a woman or her dress
denigrate-v	to criticize or belittle something or someone
denizen-n	(*literary*) a person or animal that inhabits a particular place
	The giant squid is a denizen of the ocean.
denounce-v	to accuse or condemn someone publicly
depilatory-n	a substance used to remove unwanted body hair (*also* **adj**)
deplore-v	to disapprove strongly of something
deportment-n	the way in which someone behaves in public / the way someone stands or walks
depose-v	to remove a leader or ruler from power, eg by revolution or military coup
deposition-n	a statement made under oath as required by a court of law
depraved-adj	immoral or corrupt, used of a person or their behaviour
depredation-n	(*usu* **pl**) a harmful or destructive action
	The crop has suffered from the depredations of fruit bats.
deride-v	to mock or ridicule someone or something
derogate-v	to reduce or belittle the quality of something
desecrate-v	to defile a holy or respected place, eg a grave
desiccate-v	to remove water from something or to become dry
	desiccated coconut
despondent-adj	without hope; unhappy and disheartened
desultory-adj	flitting from one subject to another; relaxed and aimless
	desultory conversation
détente-n	a relaxation of tension or hostility between countries
dew-n	drops of water that condense on outdoor surfaces during the night
dewlap-n	a loose fold of skin hanging under the neck, used of animals
dexterity-n	physical skill and speed; mental or verbal skill and agility
diagnose-v	to identify a disease or medical problem by monitoring its signs and symptoms
dialect-n	a form of a language spoken in an area, with pronunciation, words or grammar that differ from other forms of the same language (*cf* **accent**)
diamante-adj	diamante jewellery is covered with small pieces of glass that look like diamonds

diaphanous-adj	thin, delicate and almost transparent, used esp of fabrics
diatribe-n	a savage verbal attack on someone or something
didactic-adj	**1** didactic writing or speech has an educational or moral lesson
	2 very eager to teach people things, esp in an annoying way
die-casting-n	the process of making objects by pouring liquid into a mould, which sets in the desired shape
diffident-adj	shy and lacking in self-confidence
diffuse-adj	widely spread over a large area
diktat-n	a harsh order imposed on people by a ruler or conqueror
dilatory-adj	slow and causing delays; sluggish
	He has been using dilatory tactics to string out the whole process.
dilettante-n	someone who is interested in the arts but with little understanding or knowledge about them
diligence-n	care, effort and thoroughness in your attitude to work
diocese-n	in the church, the area that is under the control of a bishop
dipsomania-n	the uncontrollable urge to drink alcohol
dirigible-adj	able to be manoeuvred or directed, esp of an airship (*also* **n** = a type of steerable airship)
disabuse-v	to correct a person's mistaken idea or belief *He disabused his son of the idea of playing for Manchester United.*
disaffection-n	the state of no longer feeling loyal to a person, group or ideal
disavow-v	to disclaim any knowledge or responsibility / to plead ignorance
discern-v	to be able to perceive a difference, esp the superior quality of something
disconcerting-adj	worrying, confusing or surprising in a way that makes you uneasy
discord-n	disagreement or hostility between people
disdain-n	contempt for someone or something you feel is unimportant or does not deserve respect
disingenuous-adj	not really sincere or honest, or only pretending to be
dismay-n	extreme disappointment or sadness about something bad or unexpected
disparage-v	to discuss someone or something in an insulting and unpleasant way
disparate-adj	different in quality and type; not able to be easily compared
disparity-n	inequality between things or people
	There is a huge disparity between the rich and the poor.
dispassionate-adj	calm, reasonable and objective; not affected by emotions
disquiet-n	a feeling of worry and anxiety about something

dissent-n	a show of opposition (also **v** = to disagree strongly)
dissertation-n	a long formal piece of writing on a subject, esp as a requirement for a university degree
dissident-n	someone who disagrees with or criticizes their government, esp in a country where free speech is not allowed
dissolute-adj	having an immoral way of life, esp involving excessive sex or drugs
distil-v	to purify a liquid by heating it and condensing its vapour, eg in making whisky
diuretic-n	a drug that promotes the production of urine
docile-adj	able to be managed without difficulty, used esp of children or animals
doctrine-n	a set of beliefs and principles, esp religious or political ones
dogmatic-adj	assuming a statement is true and not open to argument / prejudiced
dominatrix-n	a dominant woman, esp in a sado-masochistic relationship
dominion-n	power or authority / the area of land controlled by a ruler
doppelganger-n	**1** a spirit that looks exactly like someone who is alive **2** your doppelganger is your double
dormant-adj	inactive or not developing, but with the potential to act or develop *The volcano had been dormant for two hundred years.*
dotage-n	(*humorous*) senility; feebleness of mind, esp in the elderly
double entendre-n	a phrase with two interpretations, one being sexual
doughty-adj	brave, determined and not easily defeated
dour-adj	serious, unfriendly or humourless
dowager-n	a woman who inherits a title or property when her husband dies
doyen/doyenne-n	an older and respected man/woman in a group or profession
draconian-adj	draconian laws are extremely harsh and severe
draft-n	a rough early version of a book, play or speech
dragnet-n	an operation to hunt down criminals in an orderly and systematic way
draught-adj	draught beer or cider is served directly from a barrel
dray-n	(*also* **drey**) a low cart without sides, pulled by a horse
dreadnought-n	a heavily-armed battleship
dressage-n	the guiding of a horse through complex manoeuvres to show the skill of the rider
droll-adj	amusing or witty, esp in an unusual or interesting way
ductile-adj	ductile metals can be pressed or moulded into shape
duplicity-n	deceit; dishonest behaviour
dyke-n	a bank that forms a barrier against water

E

earnest-adj	serious, sincere, solemn / if you say something in earnest, you mean it
earthenware-n	a pot or vessel made of earth or baked clay
earthy-adj	down to earth; coarse in manners
eaves-n-pl	the lower edges of a roof, extending past the walls
eavesdrop-v	to listen to people talking without their knowledge
ecclesiastical-adj	relating to the Christian church
eclectic-adj	an eclectic mixture of things is diverse and varied
	an eclectic mix of music, real ales, food and the arts
ecumenical-adj	relating to activities and ideas that unite the whole Christian church
eddy-n	movement against the flow, eg of water, producing a whirlpool
edentulous-adj	(*medical*) having no teeth
edict-n	an official order issued by a government or other authority
edifice-n	a building, esp a large and impressive one
effable-adj	capable of being expressed, eg in words
efface-v	to remove something or make something disappear
effete-adj	**1** worn out and exhausted / weak and powerless
	2 used about a man who looks or behaves like a woman
efficacious-adj	producing the desired result (= **effective**)
effigy-n	a likeness of someone that is used to mock or ridicule
effluent-n	liquid waste discharged from a sewage works or industrial plant
effrontery-n	bold, rude, offensive behaviour
effulgent-adj	bright, brilliant, shining
effusive-adj	expressing your feelings in an enthusiastic way
egotism-n	selfishness and excessive self-regard or self-centredness
egregious-adj	(*formal*) extremely and obviously bad
eisteddfod-n	a Welsh festival with music, singing and poetry competitions
élan-n	vivacity, enthusiasm; confidence and style
elder-n	**1** in some societies, a respected older person with authority
	2 a lay person with official authority in some Christian churches
elect-adj	(*used after noun*) chosen or elected for a job or position, but not yet in office *the president elect*
elegy-n	a poem or song expressing sadness, esp for someone who has died
elementary-adj	simple and basic / fundamentally important

elucidate-v	to clarify or explain; to give more information about something
elude-v	1 to escape from or avoid being caught by someone
	2 if something eludes you, you do not obtain or do not understand it *Sporting success eluded him. / The right word eludes me.*
elysian-adj	relating to a place or state of bliss
emancipation-n	freedom from unfair laws or restrictions, used esp to refer to women or minority groups gaining political, social or legal equality (= **liberation**)
embolism-n	the blockage of a blood vessel by a blood clot (= **thrombosis**) or by a foreign body eg air
embrocation-n	a cream or lotion rubbed on the body to relieve muscular pain
emend-v	to make corrections, esp in a piece of writing before it is printed (*cf* **amend**)
emeritus-adj	retired but retaining an honorary title *an emeritus professor of botany*
émigré-n	someone who leaves their country to live in another, esp for political reasons
eminent-adj	well-known and respected, esp professionally
emissary-n	an agent sent on a mission, eg representing a government
emollient-n	a cream or lotion rubbed on the skin to soften and soothe it
empathy-n	the ability to understand and share someone else's feelings
empirical-adj	based on experience and experiment rather than theories *empirical evidence*
emulate-v	to copy someone because you admire them and aspire to be like them
enclave-n	an area inhabited solely by a particular national, religious or racial group which is partially or totally surrounded by a different one
encroach-v	to advance or proceed beyond a limit into another's territory
endowment-n	income or assets given to a person or institution
enema-n	the forcing of liquid into someone's rectum to induce bowel movement
enfranchise-v	1 to give someone the right to vote in elections
	2 to free from slavery
Enlightenment, the -n	an intellectual movement in 18th-century Europe, which emphasized reason and science over religion
enmity-n	hostility and ill-will towards someone
ennui-n	the feeling of being tired, bored and dissatisfied
ensign-n	a flag showing a ship's loyalty or allegiance

entente cordiale-n an amicable agreement between countries (**the Entente Cordiale:** the 1904 agreement between Great Britain and France)

entrails-n-pl the internal organs of an animal or person

entreat-v to beg someone to do something, often earnestly and repeatedly (**n = entreaty**)

entrecôte-n a cut of beef from between the ribs, with no bone

entrée-n 1 an appetizer or starter eaten before the main course

2 a right or opportunity to enter a social group or institution

environs-n-pl the area surrounding a town or city

ephemeral-adj short lived, transient, fleeting

epicurean-adj relating to luxury and good living, esp good food

epiphany-n a moment of sudden enlightenment or realization

episcopal-adj relating to bishops and their practices

epistle-n a piece of writing in the form of a letter
the epistle of St Paul to the Romans

epithet-n a descriptive word or phrase for someone or something, eg the Bard of Avon refers to Shakespeare

epitome-n the epitome of something or someone is a perfect example of its kind

eponymous-adj the eponymous character in a book, film or play is the one mentioned in its title

equable-adj calm, even-tempered, not easily annoyed

equanimity-n even-temperedness; a calm, unruffled approach to life

equerry-n in the past, an official in a royal household who was responsible for the horses

equine-adj relating to horses

equinox-n either of the two times of the year when the sun is immediately over the equator, and the periods of night and day are equal (*cf* **solstice**)

equitable-adj fair and reasonable

equity-n 1 the value of a property after deduction of outstanding mortgage

2 fairness, justice, impartiality

equivocal-adj deliberately unclear or ambiguous; capable of more than one interpretation

equivocate-v to use ambiguous language in order to hide the true meaning

erudite-adj learned and knowledgeable; having read or studied widely

escalope-n a thin slice of meat with no bones in it, esp veal

eschew-v to avoid doing or using something, esp for moral reasons; to abstain from

escrow-n	money or legal documents held by a third party until certain conditions are met *The house deeds are **in escrow**.*
Esperanto-n	an invented language based on European Romance languages and intended as a means of international communication
esplanade-n	a long road that runs alongside the beach in a town, for walking along
espouse-v	to support or champion a cause
esprit de corps-n	respect and honour for one's regiment or group
Establishment, the-n	the most powerful and influential people in a country, usually associated with conservatism and maintaining the status quo
esteem-v	to consider highly and with respect (*also* **n**)
estranged-adj	relating to the ending of a friendship, esp of a married couple *He struggled to pay child support to his estranged wife.*
estuary-n	the wide lower course of a large river, where it flows into the sea
ethereal-adj	delicate, light, insubstantial; slightly unreal
eulogy-n	a speech praising someone very highly, given esp at a funeral to praise the person who has died
euphemism-n	a mild word or phrase, used to replace a more accurate but offensive one *'Massage' is often used as a euphemism for paid sex.*
evanesce-v	to fade away gradually; to vanish
evergreen-adj	evergreen trees do not lose their leaves in winter (*cf* **deciduous**)
excise-n	tax levied by a government on goods for the domestic market
excoriate-v	**1** to criticize something very strongly **2** (*medical*) to damage or remove part of the skin
exculpate-v	to prove or announce someone's innocence and free them from blame
execrable-adj	extremely bad; abominable
executive-n	a senior person in a company, with a decision-making role (*also* **adj**)
exegesis-n	(*pl* **exegeses**) the explanation and interpretation of a text, esp the Bible
exemplary-adj	excellent; providing a perfect example for people to follow
exfoliant-n	a cosmetic used to peel dead cells from the outer layers of the skin
exhort-v	to urge someone very strongly to do something *They used loudhailers to exhort people to leave the beach.*
exigency-n	a problem requiring immediate attention
expatiate-v	to develop and expand on a subject
expectorate-v	to cough up phlegm and spit it out, often noisily

expedient-n	an action that is necessary or solves a particular problem, but may not be right or fair (*also* **adj**)
expiate-v	to admit to and try to make amends for a wrong-doing (= **atone**)
explicit-adj	clearly expressed or explained; leaving no room for doubt (*cf* **implicit**)
expound-v	to expound on a topic is to talk about it in detail
expunge-v	to expunge something is to get rid of it completely, eg an unwanted written record
expurgate-v	to amend text by eliminating unsuitable or offensive parts
extant-adj	still existing, used eg of animal species and manuscripts
extempore-adj	said or done without practice or planning; off-the-cuff (= **impromptu**)
extirpate-v	to completely destroy or annihilate something undesirable
extol-v	to praise highly
extracurricular -adj	extracurricular activities are not part of the usual courses at a school or college
extraneous-adj	not relevant to an activity, subject or problem *Unfortunately the article is full of extraneous detail.*
extrapolate-v	to estimate or calculate values that fall outside the range of known values, eg by extending the curve of a graph
extricate-v	to remove someone from a difficult or unpleasant situation *She finally managed to extricate herself from the conversation.*
extrinsic-adj	not essential / existing or coming from outside a situation
exultation-n	great joy, pleasure or excitement, esp because of an achievement

F

fabricate-v	to make something up, eg a story or excuse
facetious-adj	(*disapproving*) humorous or witty, often inappropriately
facilitate-v	to make it easier for something to happen, esp something advantageous
faction-n	an organized smaller group within a larger one, esp one that disagrees with the views of the main group *political factions*
factious-adj	liable to cause conflict within a group
factitious-adj	artificial or invented / contrived or insincere

factoid-n	**1** something that is believed to be true because it has been frequently repeated, esp in the media
	2 an insignificant but interesting fact
factotum-n	a servant employed to do a wide variety of jobs; a jack-of-all trades
fait accompli-n	something that has already happened, and can not be changed
fallacious-adj	based on false ideas or information
fallow-adj	fallow land has been ploughed but not planted, esp to give the soil a chance to improve
	Each year, 75 acres are planted and 25 acres are left fallow.
farrago-n	(*disapproving*) a confused mixture of different things
	a farrago of half-truths, assertions and spin
farrier-n	a person who makes and fits horseshoes
fascia-n	a flat surface above the front of a shop, on which its name is painted
fascism-n	a political system marked by complete state control of the society and economy, no toleration of opposition and a policy of belligerent nationalism
fastidious-adj	fussy / very careful about small details; hard to please
fatuous-adj	very silly or stupid
fauna-n	the animal kingdom / all of the animals in a particular environment (*cf* **flora**)
faux pas-n	(*pl* **faux pas**) a socially embarrassing mistake or blunder
fawn-v	to seek friendship with someone using flattery
febrile-adj	(*medical*) feverish
feckless-adj	lacking determination or the will to achieve anything positive; ineffective
feculent-adj	filthy, esp because polluted with excrement or sediment
fecund-adj	very fertile, used esp of people or land / producing many good ideas *fecund imagination*
federal-adj	relating to a system of government, eg that in the US, in which the different states or regions have some self-governing powers
feign-v	to pretend or to fabricate something, eg an illness, attitude or emotion *He feigned surprise at her arrival.*
feint-n	in some sports, a quick movement intended to deceive or confuse an opponent (*also* **v**)
felicitations-n-pl	(*formal*) the expression of good wishes for someone's happiness
fellowship-n	a group of people who share beliefs or interests, eg a religious group
felony-n	(*US*) a serious crime, often involving violence (*cf* **misdemeanour**)

feral-adj	wild or uncultivated; used of animals that are normally domesticated but have become wild
fervent-adj	enthusiastic; intently serious
fetid-adj	(*also* **foetid**) decaying, esp with a rank smell
fetter-v	to bind or to restrain someone from doing something
fictitious-adj	not true or real; invented or made-up
fifth amendment, the-n	a law in the US stating that people cannot be forced to testify against themselves or be retried for a crime of which they have been acquitted
figment-n	a mental invention or fabrication *a figment of your imagination*
filial-adj	pertaining to the relationship between a son or daughter and their parents *an expression of filial duty and loyalty*
filibuster-v	to attempt to hinder legislation and the taking of a vote, esp by prolonged speaking (*also* **n**)
filigree-n	delicate, intricate designs or ornaments made from silver or gold wire
fillet-n	a boneless piece of meat or fish
fillip-n	to give someone a fillip means to give them encouragement or a stimulus
filly-n	a young female horse
film noir-n	a type of film, popular in the 1940s and 1950s, that features corrupt or cynical characters, and makes dramatic use of shadows
finial-n	a carved decoration on furniture or on the gable end of a roof
firebrand-n	someone who is very aggressive or zealous in inciting unrest and discord
firmament-n	(*literary*) the expanse of the sky; the heavens
firth-n	a river estuary, or a long inlet of the sea, used esp in Scotland
fiscal-adj	relating to government finances, esp taxation
fissure-n	a deep narrow crack, esp in rock or earth
fixtures and fittings-n	fixed and movable household furnishings or equipment, respectively. Fittings are not included in the sale of a dwelling
flaccid-adj	unpleasantly soft and limp / flabby and lacking in muscle tone *flaccid muscles and poor circulation*
flagellate-v	to whip someone usually as a religious penance *self-flagellating*
flagrant-adj	flagrant behaviour is openly offensive or immoral
fledgeling-n	(*also* **fledgling**) a young bird that is just learning to fly
-adj	a fledgeling organization is newly formed and inexperienced

Flemish-n	one of the two official languages of Belgium, the other being French
flint-n	a type of very hard greyish-black stone, used in the Stone Age for making tools (*also* **adj**)
flippant-adj	(*disapproving*) expressing an inappropriate lack of seriousness
flora-n	all of the plant life in a region (*cf* **fauna**)
florid-adj	1 a florid complexion is red
	2 (*disapproving*) flowery and over elaborate, used esp of language
flotilla-n	a fleet of small ships, esp military vessels
flotsam-n	floating wreckage or debris from a ship that has sunk (*cf* **jetsam**)
flume-n	a narrow artificial water channel, eg for transport or in a swimming pool as an attraction
flunkey-n	an insulting word for a servant or hanger-on who does small jobs for someone and behaves obsequiously
fluvial-adj	relating to or caused by a river
flux-n	1 constant change and instability
	2 the rate of flow of a substance across a given area
foible-n	a small weakness, habit or quirk in someone's character
folly-n	a whim or action that has not been thought through
	Sleeping on the beach in a high-crime area is sheer folly.
foment-v	to foment trouble, unrest or rebellion means to encourage or start it
foolhardy-adj	foolhardy behaviour or actions are undertaken without considering the risks
footloose-adj	carefree, with no ties or commitments
	Recently divorced, she was footloose and fancy-free.
foray-n	a sudden attack, raid or expedition
forbearance-n	patience and tolerance; calm, sensible behaviour
force majeure-n	1 an unexpected event or situation, eg a war, that makes it difficult for someone to carry out an obligation and can thus be used in law as an excuse
	2 an immense uncontrollable force
forensic-adj	relating to the work of scientists who investigate crimes by examining evidence such as DNA
foreshore-n	the area of the seashore between the highest and lowest points reached by the tide
forlorn-adj	abandoned and seemingly hopeless / miserable
formidable-adj	very impressive or daunting in a frightening way
	a formidable opponent

forsake-v	to leave or desert someone / to give up or renounce something that you are fond of
forthright-adj	(*approving*) direct, honest and candid
fortitude-n	strength and perseverance, esp in the face of problems or hardships
fortuitous-adj	occurring by chance, esp of a lucky event
forum-n	a place where people have a chance to air their views publicly, eg in a meeting or on TV or the internet
fractious-adj	easily angered or annoyed by trivial things; bad-tempered
franchise-n	permission given by a company to someone, allowing them to market its goods or services under licence
frangible-adj	breakable
frantic-adj	extremely worried or frightened about a situation to the point of losing control of your behaviour
fraternity-n	a group of people who share the same profession or interests
fraught-adj	to be fraught with problems or dangers means to be full of them *a journey fraught with danger*
freemason-n	a member of a secret society whose goal is to support charity and to help other members to become successful
freeway-n	(*US*) a motorway
freight-n	goods transported in bulk, by road, air or rail
frenetic-adj	frenetic activity is fast and energetic but often confused
fresco-n	a picture painted on a wall when the plaster is still wet / this artistic method
Freudian slip-n	an accidental utterance revealing an unconscious thought
friable-adj	easily broken into small pieces or made into a powder; crumbly
friar-n	a member of a religious order relying on charity or alms
fricassee-v	to cook pieces of meat or chicken in a creamy sauce (*also* **n**)
frigate-n	a small fast naval vessel, used esp to protect other ships
frisson-n	a sudden shiver of excitement or fear *The court's judgement sent a frisson of anxiety through police forces everywhere.*
frugal-adj	careful about spending money, often due to a lack of it; thrifty
fugitive-n	someone who is running away or hiding, esp from the police
fugue-n	a disordered mental state, often involving temporary memory loss and spatial disorientation
fulcrum-n	the pivot or support on which a lever turns or balances
fulminate-v	to criticize someone or something loudly, angrily and at length
fulsome-adj	(*disapproving*) insincerely excessive, used esp of praise or thanks *fulsome gratitude*

furlough-n	a leave of absence from duty, esp relating to military personnel
furtive-adj	secretive and shifty; giving the impression of having something to hide
fuselage-n	the cylindrical central portion of an aircraft, where people sit or cargo is carried
fusillade-n	1 a quick series of gunshots or of objects being thrown
	2 a rapid continuous verbal attack or series of questions
	A non-stop fusillade of questions was addressed to the president.

G

gable-n	the upper triangular part of the end wall of a building, between the sloping sides of the roof
gainsay-v	to refute or deny something
gait-n	the way that someone walks
gall-v	to be annoyed about something *Galled by her sarcasm, he hit out.*
-n	impudent boldness
	And then they had the gall to blame it all on the coach!
gallant-adj	honourable or brave, used esp of a man's behaviour towards a woman
Gallic-adj	French, used esp of character and traits that seem typically French
gallimaufry-n	a jumble or mixture of things
gallows-n	a wooden structure that is used to execute people by hanging
gambol-v	to jump around in a playful way, used esp of young animals
game-n	wild animals, birds or fish that are hunted for sport or for their meat
gamesmanship-n	the use of guile or trickery to gain an advantage in a contest without actually cheating
gamine-adj	attractive in a boyish way, used of a girl or young woman (*also* **n**)
gamut-n-sg	the complete range of things of a particular kind *In sky-diving you run the gamut of emotions, from anxiety to sheer bliss*
garish-adj	brightly-coloured in a showy, vulgar way
garrison-n	a group of soldiers stationed in a town or region
gauche-adj	clumsy and lacking tact in social situations
gaunt-adj	very thin and bony; starved in appearance

gavel-n	a small wooden hammer used by someone in authority, eg a chairman, auctioneer or judge, to get people's attention
gazebo-n	a small garden structure where you can sit and enjoy the view
gelding-n	a castrated male horse
generic-adj	1 relating to a whole range or class of similar things, eg software
	2 generic drugs are not trademarked by a particular company
gentile-n	someone who is not Jewish
gentry-n-pl	(*dated*) people of high social class
geriatrics-n	the study, treatment and care of the elderly and their illnesses
germane-adj	relevant or appropriate to the topic under discussion
germinal-adj	relating to reproductive cells / relating to the earliest stage of something's development
gerrymander-v	to change or manipulate the boundaries of an electoral area to gain an unfair advantage
gherkin-n	a small unripe cucumber, often pickled in vinegar
ghetto-n	a crowded slum area, often where a minority group lives
gibbet-n	in the past, a gallows where a hanged person was left on display
gigolo-n	a paid male escort or lover of an older woman
gild-v	to cover with a very thin layer of gold
gilt-edged-adj	1 used to refer to secure bonds, usually issued by governments
	2 excellent; of exceptionable quality
gingerly-adv	in a tentative and cautious way
gingham-n	a woven two-colour cotton fabric with a checked design
gist-n	the essential point or meaning of something
	I don't speak Italian, but I got the gist of what he was saying.
gîte-n	in France, a self-catering holiday cottage or flat for rent
gizzard-n	the part of a bird's stomach where food is broken down by muscular action and contact with small stones
glacier-n	a river of ice moving slowly under the force of gravity
glass ceiling-n	a situation in a profession where promotion appears reachable but is prevented by traditional prejudices
glaucoma-n	an eye disease in which increased pressure in the eyeball causes damage to sight and eventual blindness
glean-v	to gather bit by bit, eg information
glen-n	a deep narrow valley, esp in Scotland and Ireland
glib-adj	said easily and confidently, but often insincerely or simplistically
glitterati-n-pl	rich and famous celebrities
glockenspiel-n	a percussion instrument with tuned metal bars played by striking them with a small hammer

glossary-n	an alphabetical list and explanation of technical terms, usually at the end of a book
gluten-n	a protein found in some cereals, which some people are allergic to
gluttony-n	the practice or habit of eating too much and being greedy
goad-v	to make someone feel angry or irritated, in order to provoke them
gofer-n	a low-ranking person who does menial jobs
gossamer-n	very soft, sheer and delicate material
goujon-n	a small piece of chicken or fish, coated in breadcrumbs
gourd-n	a hard-skinned fleshy fruit, eg pumpkin or water-melon, whose empty skins are often used to carry water
grandiloquence-n	pompous and over-formal language, intended to impress
grapevine-n	the way information spreads quickly by word-of-mouth *I heard on the grapevine that she has money problems.*
grapnel-n	a metal shaft with several hooks that is used for grasping and holding objects / a light anchor for small boats
gratification-n	pleasure and satisfaction
gratis-adv	done or given free of charge
gratuitous-adj	said or done with no reason, often harmful or unwanted *gratuitous violence*
gratuity-n	a tip given for a service
gravitas-n	a serious, intelligent or impressive manner that inspires respect
greenhorn-n	an immature or naïve person
Greenwich Village-n	an area of New York, once popular with writers and musicians and now a tourist attraction
gregarious-adj	**1** living in a community or (of animals) in a flock or herd **2** friendly and sociable; preferring to be with other people
grenade-n	a small bomb that is thrown by hand or fired from a gun
grenadier-n	**1** in the past, a soldier trained to use grenades **2** a soldier who belongs to an important regiment in the UK
griddle-n	a heavy flat metal plate that is heated and used to cook food, esp batter mixtures
gridiron-n	American football, esp its playing field
grievance-n	a belief that you have been treated unfairly / a complaint about this
grievous-adj	very severe / painful and distressing
grindstone-n	**1** a revolving stone wheel that is used for sharpening tools **2 keep / put your nose to the grindstone** = to work very hard
gringo-n	an offensive word for an English-speaking foreigner, used esp in Latin America

grist-n	**1** grain such as wheat that is ready to be ground into flour
	2 grist to your mill is something you can use to achieve an aim
gristle-n	tough cartilage in meat, which is difficult to chew
groin-n	the crease between the legs and the abdomen
grotto-n	a small cave pleasantly furnished, often created artificially
	The children visited Santa's grotto.
grout-n	the filler that is used between tiles on a wall or floor
grove-n	a small plantation of trees
groyn-n	a wall perpendicular to the shore to prevent coastal erosion
guano-n	the waste matter of sea-birds, dried and used as fertilizer
guild-n	an organization whose members have the same job or interests
	the Women's Guild / the Southern Highlands Handicraft Guild
guile-n	the use of dishonest methods to deceive someone
gulf-n	**1** an area of sea partially surrounded by land
	2 a large and significant difference between people or groups
gully-n	a long narrow valley formed esp by rainwater running down a slope
gunny-n	strong coarse jute cloth used for making sacks
gunwale-n	the top edge of the side of a boat or small ship
gurney-n	(*US*) a stretcher on wheels, used in a hospital to transport patients
gusset-n	a piece of fabric sewn into a garment to enlarge or strengthen it

H

haberdashery-n	everything used for sewing and mending, eg needles and thread / a shop selling this
hacienda-n	a large estate or farm in a Spanish-speaking country
hackneyed-adj	hackneyed words or phrases have been used so often that they have become boring or meaningless
haemorrhoids -n-pl	painfully swollen blood vessels in or near a person's anus (= **piles**)
halcyon-adj	relating to a former time of peace and contentment
	the halcyon days of my youth
halitosis-n	unpleasantly smelling breath
hallmark-n	a stamp of authenticity on silver, gold or platinum
halterneck-n	a woman's sleeveless garment that ties around the neck

ham-n	an actor who performs with exaggerated or false emotion
Hansard-n	in the UK, the official published reports of parliamentary proceedings
hapless-adj	unlucky or unfortunate, used of a person
harbinger-n	a sign that something is going to happen, usually something bad *In Greek mythology, an eclipse was a harbinger of doom*
hardball-n	(*US*) baseball (**play hardball (v)** = to use all methods to achieve what you want, esp in business or politics)
harlequin-n	a mediaeval clown or comic who wore brightly-coloured clothes
-adj	a harlequin pattern consists of brightly-coloured diamond shapes
harlot-n	(*dated*) a prostitute
harridan-n	(*dated*) an unpleasant, bad-tempered old woman
harrow-n	a farming machine used to break up the soil
haunches-n-pl	the hindquarters of an animal, including the hips, buttocks and upper legs
haven-n	a place of shelter, safety or refuge
hawker-n	a street seller who carries goods from place to place
hay-n	long grass that is cut, dried and used as animal feed
hearsay-n	rumour / information you have heard but that is not necessarily true
hedonism-n	the doctrine that pleasure is the chief aim of life
hegemony-n	control or protection by one state over others in an alliance
heifer-n	a young cow that has not yet given birth
heinous-adj	very shocking or immoral *a heinous crime*
helm-n	the handle of the rudder or steering apparatus of a boat
heresy-n	opinions or beliefs that contradict established religious teaching
hermetically-adv	if something is hermetically sealed, it is completely airtight
hernia-n	a medical condition in which an internal organ bulges through a weak point in the surrounding tissue
hessian-n	a coarse strong fabric, used to make sacks or upholstery
heterogeneous	consisting of many different parts or elements
-adj	*The elderly are a very heterogeneous group* (*cf* **homogeneous**)
heuristics-n	a way of solving problems using experience, trial and error, and other informal means
hew-v	to cut wood or stone, using a tool, such as an axe *A mile of corridors had been hewn out of the solid rock.*
hiatus-n	a break or interruption in an activity, when nothing happens
hidebound-adj	(*disapproving*) narrow minded and inflexible
hierarchy-n	a system for organizing people according to rank or importance
hinterland-n	an area of land that lies beyond a developed, populated one

hippodrome-n	a music hall, variety theatre or circus
hirsute-adj	(*humorous*) hairy, used of a person
histrionics-n-pl	an exaggerated manner that is excessively dramatic, used to attract attention
hives-n	a condition in which the skin becomes red and itchy (= **urticaria**)
hoary-adj	1 old and white-haired, used of a person
	2 a hoary problem or joke is old and familiar
hobo-n	a tramp or roaming labourer
hock-n	1 the middle joint of an animal's back leg
	2 a German white wine
hoi polloi-n	an insulting word for ordinary people; 'the masses'
homily-n	a religious sermon or short moralizing speech
homogeneous -adj	consisting of parts or elements that are all of the same type (*cf* **heterogeneous**)
honorific-adj	an expression or title used to show respect for someone
hors d'oeuvre-n	a starter or appetizer before the main meal
horticulture-n	the study and practice of cultivating plants
hosanna-n	a loud declaration in praise of God
howitzer-n	a short-range cannon that fires shells at a steep angle
hubris-n	excessive pride
huckster-n	someone who tries to sell things in a very aggressive and forceful way
hue and cry-n	a public outcry
hull-n	the main frame of a boat or ship
humanism-n	the belief in humanity as a reason for morals, rather than religion
humanities-n	study of aspects adding to human culture such as history, philosophy and literature as opposed to the sciences
humid-adj	uncomfortably damp, with a lot of moisture in the air
hurdy gurdy-n	a mechanical musical instrument, such as a barrel organ, played by turning a handle
husbandry-n	1 the practice, science and management of farming
	2 economical management of a household; thrift
husk-n	the hard, often inedible outer covering of a fruit, seed or nut
hustings-n	political campaigning aimed at getting votes in an election
hybrid-n	1 an animal or plant produced by parents of different breeds
	2 a mixture of two or more different things *They produced a hybrid car capable of running on petrol or electricity.*
hydrofoil-n	a large boat that is propelled over the surface of the water
hyperbole-n	exaggeration used deliberately for effect or to impress someone

hyperspace-n	the science-fiction idea of outer space with more than three dimensions
hypertension-n	high blood pressure
hypochondria-n	abnormal worry over the state of your health

I

iconic-adj	well known as symbolic or representative of an idea or image
iconoclastic-adj	attacking established ideas and beliefs, used of people or principles
idiom-n	a phrase, the meaning of which can not be deduced from the separate words, eg 'at sixes and sevens' = a state of confusion
idiosyncratic-adj	quirky; interestingly unusual
ignoble-adj	dishonourable and shameful
ignominious-adj	an ignominious defeat or failure makes you feel humiliated
illustrious-adj	distinguished and deservedly famous
immemorial-adj	extremely old (**since time immemorial** = for a very long time)
imminent-adj	due to happen very soon (= **impending**)
immodest-adj	immodest behaviour is indecent or shocking
immunity-n	1 freedom or exemption from something unpleasant, eg a restriction *The ambassador claimed diplomatic immunity.*
	2 if you have immunity to a particular disease, you cannot catch it
impartial-adj	not personally involved in a situation, and so able to judge it fairly
impasse-n	a point at which no further progress can be made; a deadlock
impeach-v	to charge someone, esp a public official, with a serious crime
impecunious-adj	very poor (= **indigent**)
imperial-adj	1 relating to an empire
	2 relating to a British system of weights and measures that used ounces, pounds, feet etc, as opposed to the metric system
imperious-adj	giving orders in a superior way that shows you expect obedience
implicit-adj	suggested or understood rather than stated directly (*cf* **explicit**)
importune-v	to appeal to someone for something persistently
impotence-n	1 inability to act, eg because you do not have power or control
	2 the inability of a man to have sex, esp due to erectile problems
imprecation-n	cursing or swearing that is intended to bring evil

impresario-n	a producer or manager of the performing arts
impromptu-adj	unrehearsed or improvised, eg of a speech or performance
improvise-v	1 to do something without preparation, eg in music or theatre
	2 to make something using whatever tools and materials you can find
impugn-v	to verbally attack someone, implying that they are bad, dishonest or cowardly
impunity-n	freedom from punishment, esp when deserved
impute-v	to attribute a particular unpleasant event or action to someone
inane-adj	very stupid or without much sense
inception-n	(*formal*) the start, used of eg an institution or project
incipient-adj	just starting to happen or develop
	Economists fear the incipient inflation.
incite-v	to deliberately encourage people to fight or act violently
inclement-adj	severe, esp of the weather
incongruous-adj	unexpected or inappropriate in a particular situation
incorrigible-adj	(*humorous*) used to say that someone has too many faults to ever change
inculcate-v	to instil learning by frequent repetition
incumbent-n	the person who is the current holder of an official post (*also* **adj**)
incursion-n	a sudden invasion into someone else's territory
indefatigable-adj	tireless and determined never to give up
indemnity-n	protection from loss and damage, esp through an insurance policy
indict-v	to officially charge someone with a criminal offence
indifferent-adj	having no interest in something; unconcerned
indigent-adj	very poor; penniless
indignation-n	anger about an unfair situation or about being treated unjustly
indolent-adj	very lazy
indomitable-adj	having great courage and determination
ineffable-adj	unspeakable / too extreme to be spoken
inept-adj	incompetent or without skill
inertia-n	1 unwillingness or inability to change a situation
	2 the tendency of a body to maintain its position or movement until it is acted upon by an external force
inexorable-adj	an inexorable process cannot be stopped / unrelenting
infamous-adj	having a very bad reputation (= **notorious**)
infantry-n	foot soldiers
infraction-n	a breach of a rule or regulation
infrangible-adj	unbreakable

ingénue-n	a young, inexperienced woman, esp in a theatrical environment
ingenuous-adj	innocent, trusting and honest
ingratiate-v	to try hard to get someone's approval, esp by flattery
	He immediately started trying to ingratiate himself with the boss.
inherent-adj	relating to the essential, natural part of something
	the inherent beauty of a rose
inimitable-adj	unique, used esp of someone's style or way of doing things
innate-adj	a quality or ability existing from birth, rather than acquired
innocuous-adj	harmless; not dangerous or offensive
inordinate-adj	excessive, used to describe time or money
insidious-adj	developing gradually and subtly, but dangerous and threatening
insipid-adj	dull, boring / tasteless or bland, used of food or drink
insouciant-adj	carefree and unconcerned, used of someone's behaviour or manner
insuperable-adj	an insuperable obstacle or problem cannot be overcome
insurgent-n	a rebel who revolts against the government or other authority
insurrection-n	a rebellion against a government or army
intangible-adj	difficult to define or explain; abstract
integrity-n	honesty and moral uprightness
intercede-v	to speak on behalf of another in a dispute
internecine-adj	internecine conflict or warfare happens within a group or country and is destructive to all sides
interpolate-v	1 to add a comment to a conversation or a few words to a written text
	2 to estimate a value between two known values, eg of a graph (*cf* **extrapolate**)
intestate-adj	without having made a legally valid will *He died intestate.*
-n	someone who dies without having made a will
intractable-adj	very difficult to deal with, used esp of problems or conflict *intractable pain*
intransigent-adj	refusing to change your opinion about something; stubborn
intrepid-adj	very brave, esp in the face of danger
intrigue-n	a secret plot or scheme, usually to harm someone
intrinsic-adj	relating to the essential features of a thing (= **inherent**)
Inuit-n	native people of the Canadian Arctic, Alaska and Greenland (= **Eskimos**, a word now considered offensive)
invective-n	rude and abusive language directed at someone *As he ran off he let out a stream of racist invective.*
inveigh-v	to speak bitterly against someone
inveigle-v	to persuade someone to do something, esp by trickery

inventory-n	a catalogue of items, eg in a warehouse, shop or office
inveterate-adj	long-standing or deep-rooted *an inveterate gambler*
invidious-adj	likely to cause offence / falsely or unfairly discriminating
invoke-v	**1** to use a principle, law or rule to support your views
	2 to summon spirits or magical forces to help you
irascible-adj	easily upset or quick-tempered
ire-n	(*formal*) anger
irony-n	a witty form of humour in which words or facts suggest the opposite of what they actually mean. *The police car was stolen outside the police station in broad daylight.*
irrevocable-adj	impossible to change or stop; irreversible
isthmus-n	a narrow piece of land with water on each side, connecting two land masses
itinerant-adj	travelling around frequently, eg to look for work *an itinerant pedlar*
Ivy League-n	the eight prestigious universities in the north-eastern USA, including Harvard, Yale and Princeton

J

jack-knife-v	if a lorry jack-knifes, the trailer swings forward, forming a 'V' shape
jetsam-n	equipment or cargo thrown out to lighten a ship (*cf* **flotsam**)
jingoism-n	extreme patriotism; belief in your country's superiority
jowls-n-pl	the lower cheeks, esp droopy ones (**cheek by jowl** = very close)
jubilee-n	a special anniversary *the Queen's Golden Jubilee*
Judaism-n	the religion of the Jews
junket-n	(*disapproving*) a publicly funded trip for officials (= **jolly**)
jurisdiction-n	the authority to make legal judgments and enforce laws
jurisprudence-n	the science and philosophy of law / the system of law in a region
Justice of the Peace-n	a lay person who judges less serious cases in local criminal courts
juvenile-adj	relating to young people / childish or silly *juvenile behaviour*
-n	a young person
juxtapose-v	to put things, ideas etc next to each other to emphasize their differences

K

kaiser-n	a former German emperor
Kalashnikov-n	an automatic rifle made in Russia
kangaroo court -n	an illegal or unofficial court that is determined to find the accused guilty
karma-n	the Hindu or Buddhist belief that your behaviour in life determines the fate of your next life
keel-n	the central flat plate under a boat that gives it stability
keg-n	an aluminium container used for storing and transporting beer
kernel-n	the fundamental or core part of something
keynote-adj	relating to the main theme of a speech, policy or idea
kibbutz-n	a collective, self-supporting Israeli farming community
kiln-n	an industrial-sized oven for drying bricks, glassware or pottery
kilter-n	in alignment / in good working order (**out of kilter, off-kilter** = not working well)
kin-n-pl	**1** your relatives
	2 kith and kin your friends and relatives
kindred-adj	related (**a kindred spirit** = someone who shares your views) / having similar qualities
kingpin-n	the most important person in an organization, esp a criminal one
kismet-n	fate
kitsch-n	(*disapproving*) common and gaudy art that is tasteless or vulgar
kleptomania-n	the compulsion to steal things, not necessarily for gain
knapsack-n	a bag that you carry on your shoulders (= **backpack; rucksack**)
knave-n	(*dated*) a dishonest or deceitful man (= **scoundrel**)
knead-v	to press and squeeze dough to remove the air and make it ready for baking
knell-n	the slow sound of a bell, indicating a death or funeral
knoll-n	a small hill or mound
Koran, the-n	the holy book of the Islamic faith
kosher-adj	prepared according to Jewish law, used of food
kraal-n	in South Africa, an enclosure for animals
krill-n	small, shrimp-like crustaceans, the staple diet of some whales
kudos-n	admiration or praise that you receive because of something you have achieved *Countries compete for the kudos of hosting the World Cup.*

L

lacerate-v	to cut or tear, esp skin, leaving jagged edges
lachrymose-adj	tearful
lackey-n	(*disapproving*) a servile follower or hanger-on
laconic-adj	concise, brief; terse
lacuna-n	(*pl* **lacunae**) a missing part, esp from a manuscript
lagoon-n	a shallow body of water separated from a larger one
laissez-faire-n	non-interference in other people's affairs / the doctrine of non-interference by government in commerce
laity, the-n	non-professionals, esp members of a church who are not priests
lambast-v	to criticize someone strongly, esp in public
lambent-adj	softly flickering or glowing *the lambent embers of the fire*
lament-n	a show of grief, esp over a death / a song or poem expressing deep grief (*also* **v**)
lampoon-v	to ridicule someone in a humorous way
languid-adj	slow, lazy, unenthusiastic
larceny-n	(*legal*) theft
largesse-n	generosity
lassitude-n	tiredness and lack of energy
latent-adj	present but hidden, with the potential for action *Directors are aware of the latent powers of shareholders.*
latitude-n	considerable freedom to act as you wish
latitudinarian-n	someone who tolerates freedom of thought and action
latrine-n	a toilet, esp in a military establishment
latte-n	coffee made with steamed milk
laudable-adj	praiseworthy
leaden-adj	heavy, sluggish / depressing or dull *a leaden silence*
lease-n	a legal agreement setting out the terms under which a property can be rented
-v	to use a property under lease
ledger-n	a book of financial records
legacy-n	money or property left to someone in a will
legate-n	an official representative, esp of a government or the Pope
legerdemain-n	a magician's sleight of hand / deceitful cleverness
legible-adj	written or printed clearly enough to be read
legislation-n	a set of laws, or a particular law

lethargic-adj	apathetic / with little energy
levity-n	light-heartedness, esp when faced with a serious matter
levy-v	to impose or collect a tax
-n	a government tax, eg road tax or VAT
lewd-adj	relating to vulgar or indecent language or behaviour *a lewd smile*
libel-n	false and malicious written statements about someone (*cf* **slander**)
liberalism-n	a philosophy advocating freedom, tolerance, progress and reform
libertarian-n	someone who believes in individual freedom and free will
libertine-n	an immoral person, esp with regard to sexual matters, eg Casanova
libido-n	sexual desire
licentious-adj	sexually immoral or excessive
lido-n	an area of public relaxation, including an open-air swimming pool
liege-n	(*dated*) a feudal lord, owed loyalty from his subjects
ligament-n	a tough fibrous band of tissue that supports a joint or attaches bone to bone (*cf* **tendon**)
ligate-v	(*medical*) to tie something to cause constriction, eg of a blood vessel during an operation, by means of a ligature
limber up-v	to do gentle stretching exercises in order to become supple before sport
limpid-adj	clear or translucent *limpid waters*
linen-n	strong fabric made from the fibres of flax (a plant) used to make clothes and furnishings
lingua franca-n	a language used for communication between people whose first languages are different
liniment-n	medication applied to the skin to ease aches and stiffness
lissom-adj	(*literary*) slender and graceful
litany-n	a long church prayer with participation by the congregation
literal-adj	exactly as expressed, with no interpretation *a literal translation*
lithe-adj	supple and graceful
litigation-n	legal proceedings involving contesting parties
littoral-n	a coastal area (*also* **adj** = relating to the shoreline)
liturgy-n	the order and arrangement of religious worship
livery-n	the uniform of servants or people who do the same job
lobby-v	to pressurise and influence legislators to change laws or policies
-n	an organized group that pressurizes the government for change
loch-n	in Scotland, a lake or narrow arm of the sea
locum (tenens)-n	a professional who stands in for another, eg a doctor working on a ward to cover staff sickness

lode-n	a deposit or vein of metal ore, eg gold
logbook-n	an official record of the journey taken by a passenger craft
logistics-n-pl	movement, supply and organisation, esp in a military sense
loin-n	a cut of meat from the lower back and sides of an animal
loofah-n	a rough washcloth made from a tropical plant
loquacious-adj	excessively talkative
lore-n	traditional knowledge that is handed down by word-of-mouth
lorn-adj	(*dated*) lost and forlorn (**love lorn** = sad about unrequited love)
lothario-n	a seducer of women (= **libertine**)
lough-n	a lake in Ireland
lucent-adj	luminous or shining
lucid-adj	clear and understandable / mentally sound and rational
lucre-n	(*disapproving or humorous*) money *filthy lucre*
Luddite-n	an opponent of change and technological progress
lugubrious-adj	gloomy, melancholy, used of a person
lumber-n	**1** timber for building
	2 large unwanted or unused objects
luncheon-n	(*formal*) lunch
lurid-adj	garishly colourful or vivid / lurid details are graphic and shocking
lyceum-n	a public building used for events *the Lyceum Theatre*

M

macadam-n	a hard road surface made with small pieces of stone, bound with tar or asphalt (= **tarmac**)
mace-n	a ceremonial pole carried as a symbol of authority
macerate-v	to soften something, esp fruit, by soaking it in water or alcohol *macerated peaches*
machete-n	a large broad knife used as an agricultural tool or as a weapon
Machiavellian-adj	relating to political intrigue and plotting
machinations-n-pl	secret, clever and often unfair schemes, esp in politics
macramé-n	the art of making items such as belts or bags from knotted string
madrigal-n	a song for several unaccompanied voices, popular in Europe in the 16th and 17th centuries

maelstrom-n	a powerful whirlpool / a turbulent or confusing situation
magistrate-n	a lay judge in a local court who deals with less serious crimes
magnanimity-n	generosity, esp towards someone you have defeated
magnate-n	a rich and powerful person in industry, property or the media
magniloquent-adj	pompous or grandiose, used of speech
maitre-d'-n	a head waiter in a restaurant or hotel
makeshift-adj	providing a short-term, usually inferior, solution or plan, esp during a crisis
maladroit-adj	clumsy or insensitive
malaise-n	a general feeling of unease, discomfort or sickness
malefactor-n	someone who breaks the law
malfeasance-n	wrong or illegal behavior, esp by a public official
malevolent-adj	wanting to harm others / having an evil or harmful effect
malignant-adj	1 full of hate and desire to harm / associated with evil
	2 a malignant growth or tumour is cancerous (*cf* **benign**)
malleable-adj	1 able to be easily shaped *malleable metals*
	2 easily persuaded or influenced
malt-n	germinated barley, prepared for fermentation
mammon-n	material wealth, esp as a source of evil or corruption
mañana-adv	(*Spanish*) literally 'tomorrow', used vaguely to mean sometime in the future
mandarin-n	a bureaucrat with far-reaching powers
	the faceless mandarins of Whitehall
mandate-n	1 the authority granted to someone by a vote
	2 an official command given by an authority
mandatory-adj	compulsory
manger-n	a long open box for horses or cattle to feed from
mangetout-n	a variety of pea with an edible pod
mangrove-n	a tropical evergreen shrub that grows in swampy regions
mania-n	1 an intense enthusiasm or desire; an obsession
	2 a disorder of the mind leading to agitation or violence
manifest-adj	clear and obvious *Her embarrassment was manifest.*
manifestation-n	an indication that something is real / one of the different ways that something can appear
manifesto-n	a set of published political policies aiming to win votes
manifold-adj	having various different parts
	A nursing sister has manifold responsibilities.

mannequin-n	a life-size model of a person, used to display clothes
manse-n	a house provided for a church minister, esp in Scotland
mantra-n	sacred repeated words used to concentrate the mind, esp when meditating
mare-n	a female horse
marinade-n	a mixture of herbs or spices with eg oil or wine, in which meat or fish is soaked
marionette-n	a puppet with jointed limbs, worked using strings from above
market gardening-n	the business of growing fruit and vegetables to sell
marquetry-n	inlays of wood or metal, used to decorate furniture
martial law-n	the rule of law exercised by the military, usually in times of crisis
martinet-n	a strict disciplinarian, esp in the military
Marxism-n	the political doctrine that believes class struggle will overthrow capitalism in favour of socialism
mascara-n	a cosmetic substance used to accentuate the eyelashes
mason-n	a worker in stone (= **stonemason**)
masquerade-n	a masked ball / the disguise worn at a masked ball
-v	to pretend to be something or someone different
	He was a conman masquerading as a barrister
matador-n	the principal bullfighter, esp one who kills the bull (*cf* **picador**)
matinee-n	an afternoon performance of a play, film, concert etc
matriculate-v	(*formal*) to qualify for entry to a university or college
maudlin-adj	(*disapproving*) excessively tearful and sad; overly sentimental
mausoleum-n	a building containing the tomb of a famous person or family
maverick-n	someone who flouts the rules / someone with unorthodox views
maxim-n	a brief expression of a general truth, eg 'a stitch in time saves nine'
McCarthyism-n	the practice of publicly accusing someone of communist beliefs or activities, esp in the US in the 1950s
mead-n	an alcoholic drink made with honey
means test-n	a calculation of someone's income to decide their eligibility for government benefits
medley-n	a mixture or variety of things presented together
	The band played a medley of their best known hits.
mellifluous-adj	a mellifluous voice is smooth and gentle
mellow-adj	pleasantly warm, rich and relaxing, used about light, colour or music

melodrama-n	a story or play in which emotions are very exaggerated
mendacity-n	the act of telling lies
mendicant-n	a beggar / an order of monks relying on charity (*also* **adj**)
menopause-n	the cessation of a woman's menstrual cycle
mentor-n	a counsellor or personal adviser
mercantile-adj	relating to trade or commerce
mercenary-adj	interested in money in a selfish way
-n	a soldier who fights for an organisation for financial gain, not the cause
mercurial-adj	unpredictable and volatile; subject to sudden changes of mood
mere-n	(*literary*) a marsh or lake
meretricious-adj	superficially attractive or useful but actually of little value
meritocracy-n	a society based on talent and achievement rather than money or class
metaphor-n	an imaginative way of describing something by referring to a similar thing (*cf* **simile**) *She is an angel at school, but not at home.*
metro-n	an underground rail system in a city
metropolis-n	the central or most important city in a country or region
mezzanine-n	an intermediate floor, esp between the ground and first floors
Mickey Finn-n	an alcoholic drink to which a sedative has been added to make the drinker unconscious
midriff-n	the region of the body between the waist and the breasts
mien-n-sg	someone's usual expression, appearance or behaviour *He has a somewhat predatory mien.*
milieu-n	surroundings or environment
militia-n	a civilian body of troops trained for combat / an unofficial army
milliner-n	a maker and seller of women's hats
minacious-adj	threatening or menacing
minion-n	a servant or servile follower of an important person
minstrel-n	a travelling singer or musician in the Middle Ages
minutiae-n-pl	minor details; trivia
misanthropist-n	someone who does not like other people and prefers to be alone
miscible-adj	liquids that are miscible can be easily mixed together
miscreant-n	someone who does wrong or breaks the law
misdemeanour-n	a minor offence (*cf* **felony**)
misogynist-n	someone who hates women
missive-n	(*formal*) a letter, esp an official one
mistral-n	a strong cold north-easterly wind in the south of France
mitigating-adj	mitigating circumstances or facts make a crime seem less serious or more excusable

moderate-adj	**1** average in amount / not excessive
	2 holding political or other beliefs that are not extreme
mogul-n	a wealthy and powerful businessman or woman, esp in the media
moiré-n	a type of silk with a flowing, cloudy pattern (*also* **adj**)
mojo-n	a spell or charm associated with African witchcraft
molasses-n	a thick dark syrup produced from sugar
mollify-v	to soothe or calm someone who is upset or angry
monarch-n	a king, queen or emperor who rules by hereditary right
montage-n	a picture, film or piece of music composed of many pieces put together in interesting ways
Montessori-n	an educational system that aims to develop the whole child through their natural abilities and at their own pace
moonshine-n	illegally distilled or distributed alcohol, esp whisky
moot-adj	open to argument; disputable *a moot point*
morass-n	**1** an area of soft, wet, dangerous ground
	2 a complicated and confusing situation
moratorium-n	an agreed delay or suspension pending further enquiries *France declared a moratorium on nuclear testing in 1992.*
morbid-adj	**1** very interested in unpleasant things, esp death
	2 relating to disease
mordacious-adj	caustic, sarcastic and meaning to do harm
moreish-adj	if food is moreish, you like it and want to eat more
mores-n-pl	the customs and practices of a group of people
moribund-adj	near death / decaying
mortal-adj	not able to live for ever, used to describe esp the human race
mortal sin-n	in Roman Catholic theology, a serious sin that loses the perpetrator the grace of God (*cf* **venial sin**)
mortar-n	a mixture of sand, water and cement, used to hold bricks together
mortified-adj	deeply ashamed or embarrassed
mortise-n	a lock that is set in a hole in a door frame (*also* **adj**)
motive-n	a reason for doing something, esp one that is hidden or secret
motley-adj	a motley collection is a mixture of varied and unmatched things
motocross-n	a motorbike race over rough terrain
motorcade-n	a procession of slow-moving cars, esp escorting important people
mufti-n	(*dated*) civilian dress worn by military personnel
multifarious-adj	of many different and various kinds
Munchausen's syndrome-n	a psychological disorder in which someone invents symptoms of illness in order to get medical treatment
mundane-adj	dull and ordinary

municipal-adj	relating to a town, city or borough, esp with limited self-government
munificent-adj	(*formal*) very generous
munitions-n-pl	military equipment / ammunition
murine-adj	relating to rodents
muse-n	a source of inspiration for artists, poets etc
mustang-n	a small wild horse in the south-western parts of the US
mutable-adj	able to be changed into a different form
mutton-n	the meat of an adult sheep

N

nadir-n	the lowest point (*cf* **zenith**)
	His career hit a new nadir when he was passed over for promotion.
naïve-adj	tending to have a simple and trusting view of the world and human nature
naïveté-n	trusting, innocent behaviour
napalm-n	highly flammable jelly, used in some bombs that burns the skin
nape-n	the back of the neck
narcissism-n	excessive self-admiration, esp concerning one's appearance
narcotic-n	a drug that relieves pain and induces sleep (*also* **adj**) (**narcotics** = illegal drugs)
narrow gauge-n	a railway track with a narrower width than is standard (*also* **adj**)
nascent-adj	just starting to develop *nascent democracy*
natal-adj	relating to birth (**ante-natal** = before birth, **post-natal** = following birth)
National Hunt racing-n	horse-racing with hurdles and fences
natty-adj	(*dated*) neat and smart in appearance
nausea-n	the unpleasant feeling that you might vomit; queasiness
navvy-n	an unskilled labourer, esp on a building site
neap tide-n	the lowest of tide levels due to the opposition of the sun and the moon (**spring tide** = highest level when they act together)
nebulous-adj	1 unclear; without a distinct form 2 cloudy
necrosis-n	(*medical*) the death of cells in tissues, caused by disease

nectar-n	**1** the sweet liquid collected from flowers by bees
	2 in Greek mythology, the drink of the gods (*cf* **ambrosia**)
nefarious-adj	evil, dishonest or criminal
nemesis-n	**1** punishment or vengeance due according to destiny, esp deserved
	2 an opponent, enemy or continuous problem
neonatal-adj	relating to new-born babies
neoplasm-n	(*medical*) a cancerous tumour
nepotism-n	favouritism given to members of one's own family, esp in appointments to well-paid jobs
nether-adj	(*literary or humorous*) nether regions are the lower parts of the body, or the lowest and furthest away parts of a place
neuralgia-n	pain along the length of a nerve
neurosis-n	a mental disorder that makes someone anxious or obsessive (*cf* **psychosis**)
nexus-n	a connected group or series of things
niceties-n-pl	subtle details or distinctions, esp relating to correct procedures
niche-n	a suitable place or position that gives you an opportunity for success *a niche in the market for good-quality equipment*
nicotine-n	the addictive component of tobacco
nigh-adv	(*dated*) almost / (*literary*) near or soon *The end of an era is nigh.*
nihilism-n	the belief that there is no value or meaning in anything / the rejection of conventional norms and beliefs
nirvana-n	in Buddhism or Hinduism, the attainment of perfect enlightenment and serenity
nobility-n	the most privileged class in a country, with titles that are inherited or conferred by royalty
nominal-adj	**1** in name only, not in reality
	2 a nominal sum or charge is a small, token amount of money
nonchalant-adj	unconcerned in manner or appearance
non-conformist-n	a person not complying with accepted practice
non-executive director-n	a part-time director of a company, who advises rather than makes decisions
nonfeasance-n	the act of allowing a crime to happen through non-intervention
nonpareil-n	someone or something without equal (*also* **adj**)
nonplussed-adj	so surprised or puzzled about something that you do not know how to react
non sequitur-n	a statement that does not follow logically from what precedes it
notary-n	someone with the official power to make a document legally valid
notion-n	an idea, opinion or belief

notional-adj	relating to ideas / not real yet; only conceptual
notorious-adj	well-known for a bad quality, feature or action (= **infamous**)
	notorious criminal
notwithstanding -prep	(*formal*) in spite of (also **adv**)
nous-n	common sense and intelligence
noxious-adj	harmful and poisonous *noxious fumes*
nuance-n	a subtle difference in meaning, colour or tone
nubile-adj	a nubile girl is young, sexually mature and attractive
numbers game-n	an illegal lottery, esp in the criminal underworld in the US in the 1920s and 1930s
nuptials-n-pl	(*formal or humorous*) a wedding celebration

O

oast house-n	a round building with a conical roof, housing a kiln for drying hops
obdurate-adj	not moved by persuasion / hardhearted / unreasonably inflexible and uncompromising
obeisance-n	an action showing deep respect for someone
obfuscate-v	to obscure the meaning intentionally
objurgate-v	to scold or reprimand someone
obsequious-adj	excessively eager to obey someone in a servile manner
obstreperous-adj	resisting control, esp in a boisterous or aggressive way
obtuse-adj	unable or unwilling to understand things quickly
obviate-v	to make something unnecessary
	The predicted growth will obviate the need for tax increases.
Occident, the-n	the West, esp Europe and the USA (*cf* **the Orient**)
occult-adj	**1** relating to the supernatural / obscure, secret or hidden
-n	**2** supernatural forces and practices / the knowledge or study of these
octave-n	a series of eight consecutive notes on a musical scale
ocular-adj	relating to the eyes or eyesight
OEM-acr	**O**riginal **E**quipment **M**anufacturer: the company that originally manufactured a product that is now sold under a different brand name
offal-n	the edible internal organs of an animal, eg the heart and liver

officious-adj	intrusive and interfering, used of an over-zealous official
oleaginous-adj	1 oily
	2 ingratiating; excessively eager to please
ombudsman-n	an independent arbitrator between the public and companies or institutions
omnipotent-adj	all-powerful
omniscient-adj	all-knowing
opaque-adj	not allowing light through; impossible to see through
opprobrium-n	hatred or contempt; open disapproval of someone's behaviour
oppugn-v	to question the truth of something
optimist-n	someone who is always hopeful about the future (*cf* **pessimist**)
opus-n	(*pl* **opera**) a piece of classical music by a particular composer, usually numbered *Haydn's Opus 20*
Orangeman-n	a member of the Orange Order, a society that supports Northern Irish Protestants
orderly-n	a junior attendant who carries out small tasks / an unskilled hospital worker
ordnance-n	military supplies, esp weapons systems
Orient, the-n	the East, esp countries in Asia such as China and Japan (*cf* **the Occident**)
orienteering-n	a race in which competitors run across unknown terrain using a map and compass, with staged checkpoints
original sin-n	in Christianity, the natural wickedness or sin inherent in mankind, the result of the fall of Adam and Eve in the Garden of Eden
orthodox-adj	following the traditional or established ways *an orthodox Jew*
ostensible-adj	outwardly true but concealing falsehoods or hidden motives
ostentatious-adj	intended to attract and impress people *an ostentatious lifestyle*
ostracize-v	to exclude someone from a group, refusing all communication with them
outlandish-adj	strange, unusual or bizarre, used about fashions or ideas
overbearing-adj	bossy, domineering and arrogant
overture-n	1 the introductory part of a long piece of classical music
	2 an introductory proposal marking the beginning of a discussion
overweening-adj	1 very proud and arrogant
	2 excessive *his overweening ambition*
overwrought-adj	over-excited or disturbed / distraught
Oxbridge-n	a blend of the words '**Ox**ford' and 'Cam**bridge**', used to refer to both universities for academic and prestigious reasons
oxymoron-n	a phrase containing contradictory terms, eg friendly fire

P

paddock-n	an enclosed field of grass to graze horses / an enclosure at a racecourse
paean-n	a song of praise / any statement of enthusiasm or admiration
pagan-n	**1** a worshipper of idols rather than the great religions of the world **2** someone who subscribes to an ancient polytheistic religion **3** someone who is not a member of any major religion
pageant-n	a spectacular parade or procession showing scenes of a play
pagoda-n	a Buddhist temple with a series of tapering roofs
palimpsest-n	a manuscript that has been overwritten, in which the earlier words may still be readable
palindrome-n	a word or sentence that reads the same backwards as forwards, eg noon
palisade-n	a strong fence made from vertical stakes driven into the ground
pall-v	when something exciting palls, it begins to get boring or less enjoyable
palliative-adj	palliative care or treatment controls pain but is not curative
pallid-adj	pale in an unhealthy-looking way, used about someone's complexion
palomino-n	a horse of mainly Arab blood, golden in colour with a white mane and tail
palpable-adj	able to be touched or perceived *The tension was almost palpable.*
palsy-n	muscular paralysis, resulting in disability
paltry-adj	very small / not important or valuable *a paltry sum of money*
pampas-n	a type of grass / broad grassy plains in areas of South America
pamphleteer-n	a writer or distributer of pamphlets, usually on contentious issues
pan-pref	relating to all or every (eg **pan-African** = the whole of Africa)
panacea-n	a cure for all diseases or ills
pandemic-n	a disease or epidemic that spreads widely over a large area
Pandora's box-n	in Greek mythology, a box opened by the first woman, Pandora, releasing all the ills of the world / a source of troubles. Also used to refer to analagous situations
panegyrize-v	to praise someone or something extravagantly
panhandle-v	(*US*) to beg, esp on the street

pannier-n	one of a pair of baskets suspended over a pack animal, bicycle or motorbike
panoply-n	a large and impressive range or display of things
panorama-n	a wide scenic view
pantechnicon-n	a large furniture-removal van
parable-n	a simple story, esp a religious one that illustrates a moral
paradigm-n	a typical example or model of something
paradox-n	a contradictory situation that appears impossible to all scientific reason but that has elements of truth
paragon-n	someone who is perfect / an excellent example of something *She's no paragon of virtue.*
parallax-n	the apparent change in an object's position when viewed from a different observation point
paramedic-n	a member of an ambulance crew who is trained to give first aid
paramilitary-adj	organized and operating like an army, often illegally
paramount-adj	extremely important
parboil-v	to partly cook by boiling, esp potatoes
parchment-n	**1** treated animal skin that was used in the past as writing paper **2** thick yellow-white writing paper
parenteral-adj	(*medical*) used to describe drug administration by means other than oral, esp by injection
pariah-n	someone who is hated and avoided by other people in their community
parish-n	a local community, esp with its own church and priest
parlous-adj	difficult or dangerous *The company is in a parlous financial state.*
parody-n	a gross imitation with intent to ridicule or mock
parole-n	the early release of a prisoner, conditional upon good behaviour
paroxysm-n	a sudden outburst of emotion; a spasm *paroxysms of delight*
parquet-n	geometrically patterned flooring made of small wooden blocks
parsimonious-adj	frugal or mean
parson-n	(*dated*) a clergyman in the Christian church
parthenogenesis-n	reproduction by a female without male fertilization
partiality-n	unfair support for one side against another / a strong liking for something
partisan-n	a strong supporter of a political party
partition-n	the division of a country into two or more separate countries
parturition-n	(*formal*) childbirth
parvenu-n	(*disapproving*) someone who has become rich very quickly
paschal-adj	relating to Easter

pashmina-n	a woollen shawl
passé-adj	out of date; no longer fashionable
pastel-adj	delicate and pale in colour
pasteurization-n	the process of heating liquids, esp milk, to destroy harmful bacteria
pastiche-n	a work of art that combines various different styles / a composition of art, music etc that imitates another's style
pastoral-adj	1 relating to a priest's spiritual care of his congregation 2 relating to peaceful life in the countryside
patent-n	the exclusive right granted to an inventor to use his idea or invention
-adj	1 very clear and obvious (also *adv* **patently**) 2 (*medical*) unobstructed, used of an artery or other tube in the body
pathogen-n	an organism that causes disease
pathos-n	a quality in something such as a play that makes people feel pity or sadness
patois-n	a dialect used in a particular locality
patrician-n	a member of the aristocracy in ancient Rome, with rights to hold office
patriot-n	someone who loves their country and feels very loyal to it
patronage-n	support, esp financial, given by a rich person to an artist, poet, writer or a particular cause
patronizing-adj	used to describe someone who talks to you in a superior or condescending way, or their behaviour *a patronizing attitude*
peat-n	decomposed vegetable matter that can be used as fuel or compost
peccadillo-n	a small unimportant fault or sin
pecuniary-adj	relating to money; financial *a pecuniary advantage*
pedagogical-adj	relating to the principles, theory and methodology of teaching
pedantic-adj	too concerned with small details, eg in arguments
pedigree-n	an animal of pure ancestry (**mongrel** = of mixed ancestry)
pedlar-n	(*also* **peddler**) a street seller or someone who sells door to door
peevish-adj	bad-tempered and irritable; tending to complain a lot
pejorative-adj	a pejorative word, term or connotation expresses or implies criticism
pelagic-adj	relating to the open sea as opposed to coastal waters
pellucid-adj	extremely clear; transparent *the warm pellucid water*
pelmet-n	a wooden or fabric-covered board fixed above a curtain for decoration or to hide the fittings

pelt-n	an animal skin
penal-adj	relating to the punishment of criminals
penchant-n	to have a penchant for something means to have a special liking for it
pensive-adj	thoughtful, esp in a serious or sad way
penthouse-n	a large, luxurious flat on the top floor of a tall building
penultimate-adj	not the last in a series, but the one before the last
penury-n	extreme poverty
percolate-v	**1** to pass through a filter or porous substance, used esp for filtering coffee
	2 to spread gradually, used esp of information or ideas
	The news soon percolated through to the media.
percussion-n	musical instruments that you play by striking, eg drums. The percussion is the section of an orchestra that plays these instruments
perdition-n	everlasting punishment in hell / complete failure or ruin
perdurable-adj	very durable
peregrination-n	(*formal*) a long, slow journey or voyage
peremptory-adj	of an obligation or command, not able to be ignored
	There was a peremptory knock on the door.
perennial-adj	a perennial problem is continuous or arises often / a perennial plant lives for many years
perfidious-adj	treacherous, deceitful or untrustworthy
perfunctory-adj	a perfunctory action is done quickly and carelessly
pergola-n	a wooden frame that supports climbing plants, eg in a garden
peripatetic-adj	moving from place to place, esp to pursue your career or to find work
perjury-n	the act of lying under oath in a court of law
permafrost-n	permanently frozen ground
permeate-v	**1** to spread throughout a place, used of smells or flavours (= **pervade**)
	2 to pass through the pores of a membrane (**adj** = **permeable**)
pernicious-adj	having very harmful effects
perpetrate-v	to perpetrate a crime or atrocity means to commit it
perpetual-adj	continuous; never-ending
perpetuity-n	if you have or are given something in perpetuity, you have it for ever
perquisite-n	a special benefit or incentive given in addition to a regular income or salary, such as a company car (= **perk**)

per se-adv	by itself, with no reference to anything else
	The litigation, per se, is groundless and will fail.
personable-adj	approachable / pleasant and friendly
perspicacious-adj	very perceptive and astute; quick to understand a situation
perspicuous-adj	clearly understood, used of language or writing (= **lucid**)
pertinacious-adj	determined, persistent / holding obstinately to an opinion
pertinent-adj	relevant to a particular subject
peruse-v	1 to peruse something means to read it carefully
	2 to browse something casually
pervade-v	to pervade something means to spread through every part of it
	A sense of peace pervaded her whole being.
perverse-adj	delighting in being contrary to convention or decency
pessary-n	a type of tablet or device that is inserted into the vagina for medical or contraceptive purposes
pessimist-n	someone who always fears or expects the worst (*cf* **optimist**)
petrify-v	1 if something petrifies you, it terrifies you
	2 when something organic petrifies, it is turned into stone
petty-adj	1 trivial and unimportant *petty rules and regulations*
	2 unkind and caring too much about trivial things
	She called him petty and vindictive.
petulant-adj	unreasonable; impatient in a childish way
pewter-n	a silver-grey metal alloy made mainly of tin and lead
phallic-adj	relating to or resembling a penis
philanthropist-n	someone who tries to improve humanity by performing charitable deeds
philharmonic-adj	used to describe an orchestra that plays classical music, or a society that promotes its study and appreciation
philistine-n	(*disapproving*) someone who does not care about or understand literature, art or music (*also* **adj**)
phlegmatic-adj	calm and not easily excited
phonetics-n	the study of the sounds of speech
pianola-n	a mechanical piano that produces music as a result of air passing through perforated paper
piazza-n	a large open square surrounded by buildings in a town or city, esp in Italy (= **plaza**)
picador-n	a bullfighter on horseback who wounds the bull with a lance to weaken it (*cf* **matador**)
pidgin-n	a simple language used to communicate, esp in trading, but which is no-one's mother tongue (*cf* **creole**)

piebald-adj	a piebald animal has a coat with contrasting colours, esp black and white
piecemeal-adj	(*disapproving*) a piecemeal process happens bit by bit, not regularly or in an organized way (*also* **adv**)
pied-à-terre-n	a rented flat or room, usually in a city, that you use occasionally
piedmont-n	a region at the foot of a mountain range, esp in Italy
piles-n	painful swellings of the veins inside the anus (= **haemorrhoids**)
pilgrim-n	someone who travels to a holy place for religious reasons
pillage-v	to damage and steal from a place during an aggressive raid
pillion-adv	to ride pillion on a motorcycle means to sit behind the driver
pillory-v	to be pilloried means to be publicly criticized, esp in the media
pinafore-n	a sleeveless dress worn over a t-shirt or blouse
pinion-n	a small gear wheel that engages with a larger one, eg in a vehicle steering system
pinnacle-n	the highest or most successful point of something *the pinnacle of success*
pioneer-n	a traveller who goes to settle in a new country or area / a person who is one of the first to be involved in the development of new technology
pious-adj	deeply religious, often in an ostentatious way
piquant-adj	piquant food is pleasantly spicy / interesting and exciting
pique-v	to take offence; to feel that you have been insulted (*also* **n**)
piste-n	a slope of firm snow suitable for skiing on
pitch-v	if a ship pitches, it angles up and down in a rough sea
-n	**1** the pitch of a sound or musical note is how high or low it is, depending on the frequency of the sound-wave
	2 a black sticky substance derived from tar and used for waterproofing boats or roofs
pithy-adj	concise and to the point *a pithy comment*
plagiarism-n	the act of copying someone else's work and pretending it is your own
plaintiff-n	someone who brings a legal action against another in a court of law
plaintive-adj	a plaintive voice or sound is mournful and sad
plankton-n	the mass of micro-organisms that live near the surface of the sea and provide food for marine life
platitude-n	a dull, uninspiring or unoriginal remark
plaudits-n-pl	expressions of praise or approval
plebeian-adj	in the past, from a low social class; now used insultingly

plebiscite-n	a regional or national vote on an important question (= **referendum**)
plectrum-n	a sharp pointed piece of bone or plastic used for plucking guitar strings
plenary-adj	full and complete
	Congress has no plenary powers to regulate campaign finances.
pliant-adj	**1** easily influenced and controlled
	2 pliant substances are easy to bend
plight-n	a bad or distressing situation
plinth-n	a square block supporting a statue or column
plunder-v	to steal goods or money from a town, esp during a war or raid (*also* **n**)
poignant-adj	emotional, causing sadness and regret, esp associated with the past
	The sight of the coffin was a poignant reminder of her own loss.
poleaxe-n	a tool or weapon consisting of a blade and a hammer
-v	if you are poleaxed, you are very surprised or shocked
pomace-n	pulp remaining after the juice has been extracted from fruit
pontiff-n	the Pope
pontoon-n	a platform that floats on water, used to support something or to stand on
populace-n	all the people of a region or country; the population
porcine-adj	relating to pigs or resembling a pig
portent-n	a sign or warning that something bad is going to happen
portfolio-n	your portfolio is a collection of your work, eg pictures or photographs, that you use esp when applying for jobs
portico-n	a covered entrance to a building, with a roof supported by pillars
portmanteau-n	a large leather carrying case that opens out into two parts
portmanteau word-n	a word combining sounds and meaning from two other words, such as 'brunch', which comes from b**r**eakfast and l**unch**
posit-v	to posit an idea means to assume it as the basis for an argument
posterity-n	all future generations *The event is recorded for posterity.*
post-prandial-adj	(*formal or humorous*) the period just after a meal
	Post-prandial coffee is available.
postulate-v	to suggest that something is true or should be the basis for an argument (*also* **n**)
potage-n	a thick soup
potash-n	potassium compounds, used mainly in fertilizers
poteen-n	strong alcohol distilled illegally, usually from potatoes
potent-adj	having a powerful effect or influence
potentate-n	in the past, a very powerful ruler

potpourri-n	a mixture of dried flowers and leaves, used as a room fragrance
pot roast-n	a piece of meat cooked slowly in a covered pot with very little liquid
potter's field-n	a burial ground for poor or unidentified people
poultice-n	a cloth containing a soft, warm, moist substance such as clay, applied to the skin to reduce pain and swelling
poussin-n	a small chicken reared to be eaten when young and tender
pragmatic-adj	practical and responding to immediate realities rather than theories *a pragmatic approach to the peace process*
prairie-n	in the US, a large treeless area covered with grass or wheat
praline-n	sweet confectionary, made by boiling nuts in sugar
preamble-n	an introduction to something that you say or write
precarious-adj	a precarious situation is one that could easily get worse; perilous
precast-adj	precast concrete is made into shaped blocks ready for use
precedent-n	an action or decision that can be used as a model in similar situations in the future
precept-n	a general rule or principle that helps you to decide how to behave
precinct-n	in the US, a part of a city that has its own police force and fire service / an electoral district
precipitate-v	to precipitate something means to make it happen more quickly *The crisis was precipitated by risky lending practices.*
precipitation-n	(*formal*) rain, snow, sleet or hail
précis-n	a summary of the main points of something
preclude-v	to rule something out or prevent it from happening *His new job precluded him from coaching the football team.*
precocious-adj	a precocious child is very clever or mature, often used disapprovingly
preconception-n	a preformed or prejudiced idea of something
predilection-n	a fondness or preference for something
pre-eclampsia-n	a potentially dangerous condition that may develop in the late stages of pregnancy, characterized by high blood pressure
pre-empt-v	to pre-empt a planned action is to make it unnecessary or impossible by acting beforehand
preface-n	an introduction at the beginning of a book, stating its aims or content
prehensile-adj	used to describe a part of an animal, eg its tail or toes, that can curl around and hold on to things
prelate-n	a high-ranking member of the clergy, eg a bishop
premise-n	something that is assumed and used as the basis for developing an idea

prepossessing-adj	producing an attractive and pleasant impression
preppy-adj	preppy looks or clothes are neat and smart, typical of wealthy private students in the US
prerequisite-n	a requirement needed beforehand *Good grades are a prerequisite of being admitted to Oxford.*
prerogative-n	a right or privilege
presage-n	a warning or sign that something is likely to happen (*also* **v**)
prescriptive-adj	a prescriptive approach involves telling people what to do rather than describing what happens
presentiment-n	an intuitive feeling that something is about to happen (= **premonition**)
pretentious-adj	(*disapproving*) trying to seem more clever or important than you are
pretext-n	an invented reason adopted to hide the truth / an excuse
prevail-v	**1** to triumph over, usually after a contest or argument **2** to exist widely in a community
prevaricate-v	to avoid giving a direct answer or making a decision; to equivocate
priapism-n	the persistent painful erection of the penis
primaeval-adj	(*also* **primeval**) relating to a very early period in history
prima facie-adj	appearing to be true at first assessment, used eg of evidence (*also* **adv**)
primate-n	a member of the highest order of mammals, which have certain characteristics, eg opposable digits, agility, co-ordination and a developed brain
primordial-adj	relating to a very early stage in the development of the earth (= **primaeval**)
Prince Regent-n	a prince acting as sovereign in the absence of the monarch
principality-n	a country or territory that is ruled by a prince or princess
pristine-adj	extremely clean or new / pure and unspoiled *the pristine snow*
privation-n	the lack or denial of the necessities of life, such as food and shelter
proactive-adj	taking positive action rather than just reacting to circumstances
probate-n	the legal act or process of proving the validity of a will
probation-n	a period of time during which someone convicted of a crime is supervised by a qualified officer instead of going to prison or after leaving prison
probity-n	complete honesty; absolute moral correctness
proclivity-n	a fondness or inclination for something
procrastinate-v	to continually delay doing something, usually because you do not want to do it

prodigal-adj	wasting money or time in an extravagant and careless way
profane-adj	disrespectful of religion and its values
profligate-adj	carelessly wasteful of money or resources; immoral
progeny-n-pl	a person's children, or the young of an animal or plant; offspring
prognosis-n	(*pl* **prognoses**) a doctor's prediction about the progression of an illness or disease
Prohibition-n	the forbidden production and sale of alcohol in the US during the 1920s and 1930s
proletariat, the-n	in Marxist theory, the wage-earning working classes
prologue-n	the introductory part of a book, play or poem
promenade-n	a wide road along a beach or seafront, where people walk for leisure
promiscuous-adj	having many sexual partners
promontory-n	a projection of high land that juts out into the sea
promulgate-v	to promulgate a rule or law is to pass it or make it official
prone-adj	lying on your front (*cf* **supine** = lying on your back)
pronoun-n	a word like 'she', 'them' and 'these' that is used in place of a noun *Anna realized **she** had overslept.*
propaganda-n	biased information that promotes a particular view, esp that of a political party
propensity-n	a natural tendency to behave in a particular way
prophylaxis-n	treatment, such as vaccination, that aims to prevent disease
propinquity-n	the state of being near to someone or something in space or time
propitiate-v	to appease or placate an offended group or person
propitious-adj	good in a way that is likely to bring favourable results (= **auspicious**)
proprietor-n	an owner of a business
propriety-n	correct, moral and appropriate behaviour
prosaic-adj	dull, ordinary and unimaginative
proscribe-v	to forbid something officially (= **prohibit**)
proselyte-n	a new convert, esp to a religion or political ideology
prospective-adj	used to describe future roles or possibilities *Prospective candidates will be interviewed.*
prospectus-n	a document giving detailed information about a school, college or company
prostrate-adj	lying flat on the ground, face down (= **prone**) (*also* **v** *She prostrated herself before the statue.*)
protocol-n	a system of rules for correct behaviour in formal or official situations

provenance-n	the place of origin of something; the source and ownership history of a work of art or archaeological artefact
proverb-n	a short common-sense saying, eg 'a stitch in time saves nine'
providence-n	**1** wisdom and forethought taken in one's affairs
	2 a force that some people believe is responsible for what happens to them *We must trust in divine providence.*
provinces, the -n-pl	areas of the country outside the capital or other large cities
provincial-adj	**1** relating to life in areas outside the major cities
	2 (*disapproving*) narrow-minded, unsophisticated and old-fashioned
provost-n	the head of some colleges or universities in Britain
proxy-n	a person who represents another, esp voting on their behalf *I asked for instructions on how to vote by proxy.*
Prozac-n	™ a brand name of the anti-depressant drug fluoxetine hydrochloride
prudent-adj	sensible and careful in managing one's affairs
psalm-n	a sacred hymn put into song form
psychopath-n	someone with mental health problems who may act in violent or criminal ways
psychosis-n	severe mental illness that can cause delusions and loss of contact with reality (*cf* **neurosis**)
puberty-n	the early teenage years when sexual maturation is reached and the body develops adult features
puerile-adj	silly and childish / immature
pugilism-n	the sport of boxing
pugnacious-adj	always ready to start a quarrel or fight; belligerent or aggressive
pulchritude-n	(*literary or humorous*) great beauty
pullet-n	a young female chicken, esp one that is just beginning to lay eggs
punctilious-adj	very careful to observe all the rules and behave correctly
pungent-adj	strong-smelling or with a strong bitter taste
purge-v	**1** to force people to leave a party or organization on political or ideological grounds (*also* **n**)
	2 to free something from that which is thought to be harmful
puritan-n	someone who behaves according to strict moral or religious principles, and disapproves of pleasure
purloin-v	to steal
purport-v	to claim, esp falsely *The book purports to be a manuscript written in 1426.*
pusillanimous-adj	timid; afraid; cowardly

putative-adj	generally believed; accepted as the truth
	Doubts exist about his putative successor.
putrid-adj	relating to decomposing matter, esp giving off a foul smell
putsch-n	a surprise attempt to remove a government using military force
Pyrrhic victory-n	an apparent triumph, but one in which there are heavy losses

Q

QED-abbr	**q**uod **e**rat **d**emonstrandum = as has just been proved, used eg after proving a hypothesis
quadratic equation-n	in maths, an equation with variable terms raised to the power of two but no higher, eg $ax^2 + bx + c = 0$
quagmire-n	an area of soft marshland or bog (= **morass**)
quail-v	to shrink back or recoil because you are afraid
Quaker-n	a member of a Christian denomination that rejects hierarchy and formal ceremony and is committed to pacifism
quango-n-acr	in Britain, a **qua**si-autonomous-**n**on-**g**overnmental-**o**rganisation set up by the government but working independently of it
quantity surveyor -n	somebody whose job is to calculate the total cost of a construction project
quantum leap-n	a sudden breakthrough; a major advance or development
quarterback-n	in American football, the person on the attacking side who directs play on the field
quartermaster-n	1 in the military, the officer responsible for logistics for a unit 2 in the past, the officer who allocated quarters
Queen's counsel -n	when the monarch is a queen, the highest level of barrister acting for the government (= **QC**)
quicksilver-n	mercury
-adj	very fast-changing and unpredictable *quicksilver changes of mood*
quid pro quo-n	something given, not money, in return for assistance
quinine-n	an anti-malarial drug, used esp in the past
quinsy-n	inflammation of the tonsils or throat with abscess formation
quintessential-adj	representing the essence of something; being a perfect example of something *the quintessential British Sunday lunch*
quisling-n	(*dated*) someone who supports an enemy that has taken over their country

quixotic-adj	relating to unrealistic and romanticized plans and behaviour
quorum-n	the minimum number of representatives needed at a meeting for decisions to be taken and any vote to be legitimate

R

raconteur-n	someone who habitually tells interesting and amusing stories
radical-adj	**1** radical changes or differences are significant and far-reaching *the radical reform of health provision*
	2 radical opinions and policies favour extreme change
-n	someone who favours revolution and extreme actions to achieve political and social changes (*cf* **reactionary**)
rafter-n	one of the sloping pieces of wood that forms the structure of a roof
ragout-n	(*also* **ragu**) a stew of meat and vegetables
Ramadan-n	in the Islamic calendar, the ninth month, when the Koran was revealed to the prophet Mohammed and when Muslims fast from sunrise to sunset
rambunctious-adj	very noisy; cheerful and energetic
ramification-n	(*usu* **pl**) ramifications are all the consequences or effects of something *This ruling could have serious ramifications for the way banks operate.*
rampart-n	(*usu* **pl**) a strong wall built to protect a castle or city
ramrod-n	a long narrow rod used to force explosive down the barrel of a gun
rancid-adj	stale and offensive, used esp of fat that has gone bad
rancour-n	bitterness, anger or resentment
rankle-v	if something unfair or wrong rankles, you remain upset or bitter about it
rapacious-adj	selfishly greedy and grasping; always wanting more
rapier-n	a long thin sword with a sharp tip
-adj	sharp, used of wit or intelligence *her brilliant insight and rapier wit*
rapprochement-n	a renewal of good relations between countries or groups, esp after a period of hostility
raptor-n	a bird of prey with the ability to grasp with its feet, eg an eagle
rapture-n	great joy or pleasure
ratify-v	to ratify something such as a treaty is to give it official approval
rating-n	a low-ranking seaman

rationale-n	the reasons for a decision, course of action or belief
raucous-adj	a raucous voice or sound is loud and harsh
	the raucous cry of the gulls
ravine-n	a deep narrow valley with steeply sloping sides
raze-v	if buildings or villages are razed to the ground, they are completely destroyed
reactionary-n	a person who opposes social or political change (*also* **adj**) (*cf* **radical**)
realm-n	(*formal*) a country ruled by a monarch (= **kingdom**)
ream-n	a standard quantity of paper (500 sheets)
rebuke-v	to scold / to criticize someone severely for a fault (*also* **n**)
recalcitrant-adj	stubborn and unwilling to obey / difficult to deal with *a recalcitrant child*
recant-v	to say publicly that you no longer hold a particular belief
recapitulate-v	to summarize or restate the main points of a description
recede-v	to move away; to fade into the background
recidivist-n	a person who repeatedly reoffends after being punished for a crime
reconcile-v	**1** to make two apparently conflicting things compatible or consistent
	2 to bring people or groups together again after a period of hostility
recondite-adj	understood by only a few people; obscure
reconnaissance-n	a military survey of the enemy's land
reconnoitre-v	to obtain military information about an area, eg by flying over it
recreant-adj	disloyal or cowardly
recriminate-v	to accuse someone, esp in retaliation (**n** = **recrimination**)
rectitude-n	morally correct behaviour
recumbent-adj	lying down on the back or side, at rest
recuperate-v	to recover your health or strength, esp after an illness or injury
redemption-n	the state of being freed from sin and evil, esp by God or providence
redneck-n	(*disapproving*) a white American man, usually from the rural south, who is uneducated and has racist or bigoted opinions
redolent-adj	fragrant, reminding you strongly of something *The cockpit smell is redolent of a classic car.*
redoubtable-adj	respected and slightly feared; formidable; worthy
redress-n	compensation for a loss suffered or a wrong done to someone (*also* **v**)
refectory-n	a canteen in an institution *the college refectory*

Reformation, the -n	a 16th-century movement for reform of the Catholic church that led to the establishment of Reformed or Protestant churches
refractory-adj	unmanageable; stubborn and difficult to control
refugee-n	a person seeking sanctuary or safety from danger, esp from their own country
refulgent-adj	shining brightly
regatta-n	a sporting event consisting of a series of boat races
regent-n	a ruler of a country while there is no monarch
Regina-n	a word meaning 'Queen', used esp in the titles of court cases *Regina v. Derbyshire County Council*
registrar-n	someone whose job is to keep official records, esp of births, marriages and deaths / a senior administrative officer in a college or university
regression-n	a return to an earlier or less developed stage
Reichstag, the-n	the German parliament
rejoinder-n	a quick, witty or rude reply (= **retort**)
remedial-adj	relating to help and improvement, used eg of the teaching of less able students, or medicine that relieves symptoms
remiss-adj	negligent; not taking enough care
remonstrate-v	to forcibly protest about someone's behaviour
remorse-n	a strong feeling of regret and shame about something you have done
remunerate-v	(*formal*) to pay for goods or services
Renaissance, the -n	in Europe, the period between the 14th and 17th centuries, when art and literature flourished, and there were important scientific advances
rend-v	(*dated*) to tear or split something
render-n	a layer of plaster or cement spread onto a wall, as decoration or for protection (*also* **v**)
renegade-n	a person who changes sides in a conflict
renege-v	(*also* **renegue**) to renege on a promise or deal is to go back on your word
renitent-adj	reluctant to give in or change your mind
renovate-v	to repair and restore a building, old furniture, artwork etc
repertoire-n	all the songs, poems or plays that someone knows and can perform / all the skills that someone has
repertory-n	a collection of plays or songs performed by a particular company / the place for storage of such a collection
reprehensible-adj	reprehensible behaviour is wrong or immoral

reprimand-n	a sharp rebuke by someone in authority (*also* **v**)
reprisal-n	a violent or harmful punishment imposed in revenge or retaliation
reproach-v	to blame someone or express disapproval of their behaviour (*also* **n**)
reprobate-n	a person who behaves in an immoral or incorrect way
reprove-v	to scold someone
republic-n	a country with an elected government, led by a president
rescind-v	if a decision, law or contract is rescinded, it is withdrawn or cancelled
resounding-adj	loud, clear or unmistakable *a resounding success*
restive-adj	restless, due to waiting / unwilling to move forward
reticent-adj	disinclined to put yourself forward; reserved
retinue-n	a group of people attending to the needs of a dignitary or person of wealth (= **entourage**)
retort-n	a quick, witty or rude reply (*also* **v**) (= **rejoinder**)
retrench-v	to economize; to cut back on spending
retribution-n	punishment for an offence, esp through unofficial acts of revenge
retrospection-n	the reassessment of past events
reveille-n	a bugle call to awaken or summon troops / the time of day this is sounded
reverence-n	**1** great respect for someone or something **2** religious devotion
revoke-v	to revoke a law, licence or agreement is to withdraw or cancel it
rhapsody-n	an emotional musical composition with an irregular form
rhetoric-n	eloquent speech, used to persuade or influence people
rhetorical question-n	a statement made as a question for effect, but that does not require an answer
rhinestone-n	a glittery glass stone used in costume jewellery and for decorating clothes; an imitation diamond
Rhode's scholar -n	a student from the US, South Africa or a Commonwealth country who has won a scholarship to Oxford University
ribald-adj	obscene and coarse, used of language *ribald jokes*
rickshaw-n	a light two-wheeled passenger vehicle that is pulled by a bicycle or someone on foot
rictus-n	a fixed unnatural grimace or grin, esp in horror or death
rigour-n	**1** severity, strictness or harshness **2** if something is done with rigour, it is done in a thorough, precise way
ring fence-v	to specify that a fund or grant be used for one particular purpose

riposte-n	a quick witty reply, esp to criticism
risible-adj	ridiculous, laughable; not to be taken seriously
	The insurer's offer of compensation was risible.
roan-n	a horse with a brown or black coat speckled with white hairs
	(*also* **adj**)
rococo-n	an elaborate 18th-century ornamental decorative style with a
	propensity for swirls, curves and shell motifs
Rosh Hashanah-n	the Jewish new year festival
rostrum-n	a platform for speakers or for an orchestral conductor
roundly-adj	thoroughly / without tact *He was roundly criticized by the media.*
roustabout-n	(*dated*) an unskilled labourer, esp at a port or oilfield
Rubicon-n	to cross the Rubicon is to take a step that commits you to a course of
	action (**the Rubicon** = the stream crossed by Julius Caesar in 49 BC)
rubicund-adj	(*literary*) red-faced in a healthy way; ruddy
rubric-n	**1** a set of instructions, eg in an exam or textbook
	2 a title, heading or initial letter, eg in a legal document
ruche-n	a strip of gathered or pleated fabric that falls in soft folds
ruction-n	(*usu pl*) a quarrelsome or noisy confrontation
rune-n	a character in one of many Germanic alphabets used between
	the 3rd and 13th centuries. Runes were believed to have magical
	significance
rustic-adj	rural in a simple old-fashioned way

S

sabbatical-n	a period of paid leave from a job, esp for travel or study
	It's my third week on sabbatical.
sacrament-n	a Christian ceremony such as baptism or marriage / **the**
	Sacrament = the bread and wine taken at an Anglican
	communion service
sacrilege-n	behaviour showing great disrespect for something considered holy
	or sacred
sacrosanct-adj	so special as to be beyond threat or criticism
	The rights that protect our liberty are sacrosanct.
sage-n	a wise person, used esp of someone who is old and has a lot
	of experience

salacious-adj	showing an excessive interest in sex and eroticism
salient-adj	prominent, crucial or most noticeable
	the salient points of his speech
sallow-adj	pale and yellowish in an unhealthy way, used esp of someone's complexion
salubrious-adj	**1** beneficial to health
	2 pleasant, clean and healthy, often used humorously about a place
salutation-n	(*formal*) a greeting
salve-n	a thick ointment for soothing the skin
-v	to save something from destruction (**n = salvage**)
salvo-n	the simultaneous firing of several guns or missiles, esp in a ceremony
sanatorium-n	a place for medical care and recuperation, esp for long-term patients
sanctimonious-adj	(*disapproving*) excessively pious and self-righteous
sanctuary-n	a place where people or animals can be protected from persecution or danger *a bird sanctuary*
sang froid-n	composure and calmness under pressure or in a dangerous situation
sanguine-adj	**1** optimistic and confident, esp about future progress or outcomes
	2 red in appearance
sanitary-adj	relating to clean, healthy conditions and the prevention of infection
Sanskrit-n	an ancient classical language used in India and preserved in literary and religious texts
sapid-adj	palatable or agreeable / not dull
sapient-adj	learned, wise and knowledgeable
Saracen-n	an old word for a Muslim, esp someone who fought in the mediaeval Crusades
sarcastic-adj	mocking; saying the opposite of what you mean in a witty and unkind way *He made mocking and sarcastic remarks.*
sardonic-adj	(*disapproving*) cynically mocking; showing contempt for someone
sartorial-adj	relating to clothes and tailoring *sartorial elegance*
sash window-n	a window that opens from the top or the bottom, consisting of two frames that slide over each other in vertical grooves
satiate-v	to satisfy an appetite or craving
satire-n	exaggerated humour or mockery that shows the faults of something / a play or novel that uses this type of humour

sauté-v	to cook food by frying it gently in hot oil (*also* **adj**)
savant-n	a very knowledeable person
savoir faire-n	the ability to do the right thing in a situation
scabbard-n	a sheath for the blade of a sword or dagger, that hangs from a belt
scarp-n	a steep slope or cliff, usually formed by erosion
sceptic-n	a person who doubts commonly accepted beliefs
Schadenfreude-n	the feeling of pleasure that someone has at another's misfortune
schism-n	the separation of a group into two factions, used esp of religious splits
schmaltz-n	excessive sentimentality
schnitzel-n	a thin piece of meat, esp veal, coated with breadcrumbs and fried
sciatica-n	severe pain from the lower back to the calf, running along the sciatic nerve
scimitar-n	a short sword with a curved blade that broadens towards the point
scion-n	**1** one of the younger members of a famous or wealthy family **2** a cutting from a plant, used for grafting
scorn-n	open contempt for someone or something (*also* **v**)
scree-n	the accumulation of loose stones at the base of a cliff or mountain
scriptures-n	the sacred writings of a religion (**the Scriptures** = the Christian Bible)
scruple-n	(*usu* **pl**) a moral principle or belief that prevents you from doing wrong *His lack of scruples made him a sought-after barrister.*
scuba diving -n-acr	diving in deep water using **S**elf-**C**ontained **U**nderwater **B**reathing **A**pparatus, a canister of air carried on the back and inhaled through a mouthpiece
scurrilous-adj	untrue and unfair, damaging to someone's reputation *scurrilous attacks on the president*
scuttle-v	to cause a vessel to sink by making a hole in it
scythe-n	a long-handled curved blade, used to cut long grass or grain (*also* **v**)
secession-n	the formal separation of a group or region from a larger one (**v** = **secede**)
sectarian-adj	**1** belonging to a religious group **2** narrow-minded and bigoted
secular-adj	relating to worldly matters, not religious
sedative-n	a drug producing a calm or sleepy effect (*also* **adj**)
sedentary-adj	a sedentary life-style or job involves a lot of sitting and little exercise
sedition-n	language or behaviour that encourages public disorder
seemly-adj	seemly behaviour or dress is appropriate for the occasion

segue-v	to move smoothly and seamlessly from one thing to another (*also* **n**)
self-deprecating -adj	self-critical, modest; tending to belittle yourself
self-effacing-adj	unwilling to draw attention to yourself or your achievments
semantic-adj	relating to the meaning of words
semester-n	in some countries, esp the US, one of the two periods that the academic year is divided into
seminal-adj	very important and influential, used esp of ideas, books or events
seminar-n	a small class, esp in higher education, that meets for discussion and learning with a tutor
senate-n	**1** the smaller and more important of two elected legislative bodies in some countries, eg the US, Australia, and France **2** the main governing body in some colleges and universities
senile-adj	forgetful, confused or mentally less acute in later life
sententious-adj	(*disapproving*) pompous and moralistic, used of language
sentient-adj	able to feel and to experience things through the senses
sentinel-n	(*dated*) a guard (= **sentry**)
separatist-n	someone who wants their group or region to become independent and self-governing
sepia-n	a dark reddish-brown colour, characteristic of old photographs
sepoy-n	in the past, an Indian soldier under British command
septicaemia-n	blood poisoning caused by toxic micro-organisms
sepulchre-n	a stone burial tomb, used for an important person
sequester-v	to remove from the main body, usually for a period of time
serendipity-n	the event of finding something pleasant or valuable when you least expected to
serenity-n	calmness, peace
serpentine-adj	winding and twisting like a snake, used eg of a path
serrated-adj	having a sharp jagged edge like the teeth of a saw
servile-adj	(*disapproving*) behaving in a fawning or obsequious way
servitude-n	the condition of being a slave or being under someone's control
servo-adj	relating to a device that amplifies or corrects a mechanical input, such as the steering or braking of a vehicle
sessile-adj	(*formal*) permanently attached rather than free moving, used of an animal such as a barnacle / a sessile flower has no stalk
shaman-n	a religious leader who is believed to communicate with the spirit world and have healing powers
Shangri-la-n	an imaginary paradise on earth

sheer-adj	**1** complete; used before a noun to emphasize a quality or feature *I hadn't been prepared for the sheer size and splendour of the house.*
	2 a sheer drop or cliff is so steep as to be almost vertical
	3 sheer fabric is thin, fine and almost transparent
shin-n	the front part of the lower leg, or the bone (= **tibia**) there
shogun-n	a military leader in feudal Japan
short shrift-n	if someone gets short shrift, they are treated harshly or given little attention
showboat-v	to try to impress people by your skill or cleverness; to show off
shrapnel-n	splinters of a bomb or bullet that are scattered when it explodes
shrew-n	(*dated*) an insulting word for a bad-tempered woman
shrewd-adj	astute or sharp, esp in financial matters
shrill-adj	a shrill voice or sound is high, piercing and unpleasant
Shylock-n	a money-lender with little conscience when recovering debt, from a character in Shakespeare's *The Merchant of Venice*
sibling-n	a brother or sister
sic-adv	(*formal*) 'thus', used after a word you are quoting, to show that you have copied it exactly from the original, even if it appears mistaken *I write to advice [sic] you that I am the new landlady.*
sidereal-adj	relating to the stars
sidewinder-n	a short-range US heat-seeking air-to-air missile
siding-n	a side track on a railway used for storage or as a passing place
siege-n	the surrounding of a place by an army or the police in order to force people to surrender
siesta-n	a short sleep taken in the afternoon in hot countries
signage-n	signs used on shops, roads etc / the design and display of signs *Projects include installing traffic lights and improving signage.*
signet-n	a small seal, esp one engraved into a ring, hence **signet ring**
silage-n	a green crop that is stored in very large containers as winter food for animals
silo-n	**1** a tall round tower used to store grain or animal feed
	2 an underground stronghold used for storing and launching missiles
simian-adj	relating to or resembling monkeys and apes
simile-n	an expression comparing two people or things using 'as' or 'like', eg 'as white as a sheet' or 'he dances like an elephant' (*cf* **metaphor**)
sinecure-n	a paid job with little work and few responsibilities

sinew-n	a tendon that connects muscle with bone / a source of strength
sinister-adj	menacing; ominous; threatening evil or harm
sinuous-adj	relating to curves or waves
sinus-n	an air-filled cavity in the bones of the face or skull, esp the bone behind the nose
sire-n	the male parent of an animal, esp a horse (*also* **v**)
sirloin-n	a lean, tender cut of beef, above the loin or back of an animal
sirocco-n	a hot dusty wind blowing from the Sahara desert to southern Europe
skid row-n	1 a poor and rundown part of a city
	2 if someone is on skid row, they have slipped into homelessness, poverty or substance abuse
slander-n	untrue spoken statements about someone, motivated by a desire to harm their reputation (*cf* **libel**)
sleet-n	partly frozen rain / a mixture of rain and snow (*cf* **hail**)
sleight of hand-n	skilful deception using quick hand movements in a magic trick / the use of clever tricks and lies to deceive someone
slew-v	to twist away from the normal or intended position
	The derailed carriages were slewed across the platform.
slough-v	to discard outer dead layers of skin (*also* **n**)
sloven-n	(*dated*) a person who is unkempt and careless about their appearance
sluice-n	an artificial channel for water to flow along, operated by a valve or gate, eg to get rid of waste fluids in a hospital
slush fund-n	an amount of money put aside for bribing officials, esp in politics
smallholding-n	a plot of land for small-scale farming
smirch-v	to spoil something or make it dirty, eg by staining it / to damage someone's reputation
smite-v	(*dated*) to hit someone very forcefully
smock-n	a long loose overshirt worn eg by artists to protect their other clothing
smog-n-acr	a mixture of **sm**oke and f**og** and other airborne pollutants
smokescreen-n	something done or said to hide the truth and conceal someone's real motives *They traded behind a sophisticated smokescreen of bogus paperwork.*
smorgasbord-n	(*Scand*) a buffet meal consisting of a variety of hot and cold dishes
snare-n	a trap, used to catch birds and small animals (*also* **v**)
snide-adj	sneering and derogatory, often in an indirect way
	I endured constant snide remarks from colleagues.

soakaway-n	a conduction system of waste water to the ground, rather than to a sewer system
sobriety-n	serious, thoughtful behaviour or attitudes / the state of not being drunk
sobriquet-n	an unofficial or humorous name for someone or something; a nickname
social democracy -n	the political belief that capitalism can be replaced by a system combining socialism with democratic ideals, eg elected government
socialism-n	a political and economic system based on public ownership and the equal distribution of power and wealth
socialite-n	someone who goes to a lot of parties and is well-known in fashionable circles
soda-n	a compound containing sodium esp those used around the house, eg bicarbonate of soda = baking soda
soda water-n	fizzy water charged with carbon dioxide, often used as a mixer with alcoholic drinks
soffit-n	the horizontal board that connects the bargeboard to the wall under the eaves of a roof / the underside of an arch or flight of stairs
soirée-n	a social gathering or party held in the evening
sojourn-n	a short stay away from your home
solace-n	comfort, often given in a time of distress
solemn-adj	serious and sincere *a solemn promise*
solicit-v	to ask for money, help or information / to offer sex in return for money
soliloquy-n	a solo speech in a play in which a character conveys his or her thoughts to the audience
solstice-n	the shortest and the longest day, when the earth's tilt changes direction (*cf* **equinox**)
solvent-adj	having enough money; not bankrupt
-n	the liquid in which a solid dissolves
sombre-adj	solemn and gloomy / dark, with no bright colours
somnambulism-n	(*formal*) sleepwalking
sonata-n	a classical music composition for a single instrument, or a piano and another instrument
sonorous-adj	deep and rich-sounding
soothsayer-n	(*dated*) a fortune-teller
sop-n	(*dated*) an insulting word for a weak and silly person, esp a man

sophistry-n	the practice of using clever, plausible arguments that are actually false
sophomore-n	in the US, a second-year student in high school or college
Sorbonne, the-n	part of the prestigious University of Paris
sordid-adj	dirty and squalid / immoral or dishonest
sorority-n	in the US, a society for women in a college or university
sorrel-adj	reddish-brown in colour, used esp of an animal
sortilege-n	sorcery or prediction by casting lots
sot-n	a drunkard
soundbite-n	a short extract of a speech given as a summary of its style and content, esp for radio or television
soupçon-n	a very small amount, often used humorously
souse-v	to immerse something such as a fish in liquid, esp to preserve it
sou'wester-n	a waterproof hat with a wide brim at the back to keep the neck dry, worn esp by seamen
sovereign-n	the head of state of a region, with supreme power
Spanish Inquisition, the-n	a tribunal that maintained Catholicism in mediaeval Spain, by the oppression of non-believers
spartan-adj	relating to a simple, austere way of life
spawn-n	**1** a jelly-like mass of eggs of fish, frogs or other aquatic animals **2** an insulting word for someone's children
specious-adj	seeming to exist or be true, but flawed or false *a specious argument*
speculate-v	**1** to guess what will happen in the future or to guess the reasons for something happening **2** to buy stocks and shares with a view to making a profit
spendthrift-n	someone who spends too much money in a careless way
sphincter-n	a ring of muscle that expands or contracts to control a passage in the body, eg the muscles of the anus
spigot-n	a tap that controls the flow of liquid from a container / a plug or stopper
spile-n	a wooden peg used to control the flow of carbon dioxide from a cask
splenetic-adj	bad-tempered, malicious and spiteful
splint-n	a long stiff support used to immobilize a broken bone while it heals
sporadic-adj	happening from time to time, but not regularly or predictably *Sporadic fighting continued today after the ceasefire came into effect.*

sportsmanship-n	fair, polite, honest behaviour in sports games and competitions
spouse-n	your husband or wife
sprain-n	a twisting injury of a joint, esp with damage to ligaments, tendons or muscles (*also* **v**) (*cf* **strain**)
spreadsheet-n	a computer program that displays numbers and performs calculations / a document displaying the results of this
spree-n	a social outing in which someone drinks or spends excessively
sprocket-n	a wheel with projecting teeth that engages and pulls or is pulled by a chain
spry-adj	active and energetic, used esp of an old person
spume-n	foam on the surface of a liquid, esp the sea
spurious-adj	false and incorrect, used esp of unfounded arguments and claims
squall-n	a sudden strong wind that may cause a short violent storm
squalor-n	filthy conditions, used esp of how someone lives
squire-n	in the past in England, an important rural landowner
staid-adj	of serious character / old-fashioned
Stakhanovism-n	in the former USSR, a system for increasing production through hard work and incentives
stalking horse-n	someone whose role is to hide someone else's true ambitions, esp a candidate who has no real intention of competing in an election
stallion-n	a fully-grown male horse, esp one used for breeding
stalwart-n	a strong, reliable, loyal and hard-working person (*also* **adj**)
stammer-v	to talk with difficulty, esp repeating the initial sounds of words (*also* **n**) (= **stutter**)
stanchion-n	a strong upright bar used as a support
staple-n	an essential food that is used all the time, such as potatoes or rice
-adj	used to describe something that is essential for people's lives
stark-adj	basic or austere in comfort
status quo-n	the existing state of affairs, esp one that people want to maintain
statute-n	an enforceable law
stead-n	the place or position taken by someone on behalf of a person who cannot be there *He represented the company at the conference in another person's stead.*
steadfast-adj	steady and unswerving in a belief or course of action / faithful and loyal
steeplechase-n	a long race in which horses jump over obstacles
stenosis-n	(*medical*) abnormal narrowing of a bodily passage, eg a blood vessel

stent-n	(*medical*) a tube used to keep a bodily passage such as the oesophagus unobstructed
steppe-n	a large area of flat grassy treeless land, esp in northern Asia (*cf* **taiga**; **tundra**)
sterling-adj	very good, used esp to describe someone's work or qualities
stevedore-n	a person whose job is to load and unload ships
stilted-adj	used to describe a formal, stiff, unnatural way of speaking or writing
stipend-n	a regular income, esp money paid to the clergy
stockade-n	a strong fence of wooden posts built around an area to keep animals from escaping
stoicism-n	patience and composure in the face of misfortune or during a crisis
stolid-adj	(*disapproving*) unexcited, showing little reaction to situations
strain-n	a muscle injury caused by over-exertion or over-stretching (*cf* **sprain**)
strait-n	1 a narrow strip of sea that joins two larger bodies of water *the Strait of Gibraltar*
	2 **be in dire straits** = to be in a difficult or desperate situation
strategy-n	a plan or series of planned actions with a particular aim or purpose
straw poll-n	an unofficial survey of a group of people to gauge opinion
stricken-adj	very seriously affected by something such as illness or disaster
strident-adj	forceful and opinionated in an annoying way / loud and unpleasant
strife-n	conflict; struggle; strong disagreement
stringent-adj	stringent rules, controls or conditions are very strict and severe
stucco-n	a type of weatherproof plaster used to cover external walls and to decorate ceilings
stultifying-adj	boring, tedious
stupor-n	a state of near-unconsciousness, due esp to excessive alcohol or drugs *a drug-induced stupor*
stymie-v	to obstruct or impede someone's progress (= **thwart**)
suave-adj	confident, elegant and stylish / pleasant but in an insincere way
subdue-v	to overcome and control someone, esp by force
subjugate-v	to conquer a group or nation by taking complete control
sublime-adj	excellent; worthy of the highest praise
subliminal-adj	influencing your thoughts and opinions without your being conscious of it
submissive-adj	obedient; compliant with somebody else's wishes

suborn-v	to make someone perpetrate an illegal act, eg to make a witness tell lies in court
subpoena-n	a legal document requiring someone to attend a court of law (*also* **v**)
sub rosa-adv	in secret *The meeting will be sub rosa.*
subservient-adj	obedient; too eager to follow the wishes of others
subsidence-n	the sinking of a building due to the ground giving way, often causing structural damage
subsidiary-adj	(*formal*) connected with but secondary to something else; auxiliary
subsistence-n	the state of having just enough money and food for basic survival
substantive-adj	important, real, weighty *Substantive changes must be made to the original proposal.*
subsume-v	to include something within a larger group or category so that it no longer has a separate identity *A wide range of policies is subsumed under the term 'flexible working practices'.*
subterfuge-n	a deception, aimed at hiding something
suburban-adj	**1** relating to residential areas away from the centre of a city **2** (*disapproving*) boring and narrow-minded
subversive-adj	acting to undermine or overthrow a government or state
succour-n	help given to those in difficulty or distress (*also* **v**)
suet-n	solid fat from the abdomen of a sheep or cow, used in cooking and making tallow
suffrage-n	the right to vote in elections
suffuse-v	to gradually spread through someone or something, used esp of a colour or a feeling
sullen-adj	silent and bad-tempered; surly and resentful
sultry-adj	**1** hot and humid, used of the weather **2** attractive in a sexy sensual way
summary-n	a shortened version of something, giving the main facts
summit-n	**1** the top of a mountain **2** important talks between governments *the G7 summit*
sumptuous-adj	impressive, luxurious and expensive; lavish
sunder-v	(*literary*) to split or break into parts
sundries-n-pl	a large number of miscellaneous small items *suppliers of office sundries*
sundry-adj	various, diverse
supercilious-adj	(*disapproving*) superior and arrogant; looking down on other people
superfluous-adj	more than is wanted or needed; surplus to requirements

supernumerary -adj	extra; more than the usual number, used eg of extra staff
supplant-v	to take the regular place of someone, esp by ingenuity
suppository-n	a small solid medication inserted into the rectum, that melts at body temperature
surety-n	money or goods put up as a guarantee / someone who acts as a guarantor
surfeit-n	an excess of something; much more than is needed *The internet has created a surfeit of information.*
surly-adj	rude and bad-tempered; ungracious
surmise-n	a guess based on the available evidence (*also* v)
surreal-adj	referring to a situation that is so weird and far-fetched that it appears like a dream
surreptitious-adj	done by stealth or in secret in order to deceive
suss-v	(*also* **suss out**) to find something out about someone or something, esp using one's intellect
svelte-adj	slim, elegant and graceful; lithe
swarthy-adj	dark-skinned, used esp of someone's face
sweetbread(s)-n	offal from the thymus or pancreas of a calf or lamb, cooked and eaten
sybarite-n	someone who likes to indulge in luxury
sycophant-n	someone who flatters powerful people to gain advantage
sylvan-adj	(*literary*) relating to woods or trees
symbiosis-n	a partnership between two different organisms that benefit or are dependent on each other
symphony-n	a classical music composition for orchestra, often in four movements
symposium-n	a conference for professionals in a particular subject
syndrome-n	(*medical*) a collection of signs and symptoms that characterize a disease or condition, such as Down's syndrome
synergy-n	the co-operation of two things to produce an overall greater effect than would be possible by each one working separately *Zinc aids the immune system, working in synergy with vitamin A.*
synonym-n	a word that means the same, or almost the same, as another word in the same language
synopsis-n	a short account, esp of the plot of a book or film, giving the main points
syntax-n	the way words combine to make larger grammatical units / the grammatical rules based on this

systematic-adj	applying an organized set of rules / methodical
systemic-adj	affecting the whole of something such as the human body or an organization
	The case represents a systemic failure of the legal system.

T

tabard-n	a short-sleeved or sleeveless shirt worn by a knight over his armour
tableau-n	(*pl* **tableaux**) a picturesque display depicting an event from history
table d'hôte-n	a set menu with a fixed price (*cf* **à la carte**)
tachometer-n	a device used to measure speed, esp fitted to a vehicle
tacit-adj	implied or understood but not spoken aloud
	We had a tacit agreement.
taciturn-adj	someone who is taciturn speaks very little, and appears unfriendly
tact-n	the ability to be diplomatic and to avoid upsetting anyone
tactic-n	(*usu* **pl**) the detailed and immediate methods used to achieve something
tactile-adj	relating to the sense of touch / liking to touch people
taffeta-n	a shiny silk fabric, used esp to make women's clothes
taiga-n	subarctic coniferous forests, between the tundra and the steppe
talisman-n	a charm that is believed to protect the wearer from harm
tallow-n	animal fat, used to make grease, candles or soap
tangent-n	a line or curve that touches another line or curve without crossing it
tangible-adj	clear; definite enough to be seen or felt
tannoy-n	a loudspeaker system, used to make announcements at public events
tantalize-v	to excite someone by offering them something they cannot have; to tease
tantamount-adj	equivalent to or having the same effect, as something
	The second goal was tantamount to winning the championship.
tapas-n-pl	(*Spanish*) a selection of small dishes served with drinks or as appetizers
tapestry-n	a heavy woven cloth with depictions of scenes, often hung on the walls of stately homes
tardy-adj	(*formal*) late

tare-n	the package or vehicle weight, subtracted from the total in order to evaluate the tax due on goods
tariff-n	a tax paid on imported goods / the rate charged for services such as gas and electricity, or for accomodation
tarpaulin-n	a heavy waterproof sheet, used to protect things from rain
tarry-v	(*literary*) to remain in a place for longer than is necessary
tattoo-n	a military display performed as an entertainment
tawdry-adj	cheaply and badly made; tacky / unpleasant or immoral; vulgar
tawny-adj	pale orange-brown in colour, used of hair, fur or skin
technicality-n	a point based on the strict interpretation of a law or rule / a nuance or detail of a device
tedious-adj	boring, tiring or frustrating, used esp of a job or task
teethe-v	when a baby is teething, his or her first teeth are growing
tele-pref	over a great distance (**teleshopping** = ordering goods over the internet)
temperance-n	1 (*dated*) the avoidance of alcohol, esp for religious or moral reasons 2 moderation and self-restraint
temperate zone-n	the mild climate areas between the tropics and the polar regions
temerity-n	rashness; boldness without thought for the consequences *He had the temerity to question the motives of the chief executive.*
tempest-n	(*literary*) a violent storm
temporal-adj	relating to worldly as opposed to religious matters / relating to time
tenable-adj	able to be maintained or defended, used esp of an argument or belief
tenacious-adj	unwilling to give up; persistent and determined
tendentious-adj	expressing a strong and controversial opinion
tender-v	to make a formal offer, eg to tender your resignation
tendon-n	a band of fibrous tissue connecting a muscle to a bone or cartilage (*cf* **ligament**)
tenet-n	a belief or principle, esp one that is part of a religion or philosophy
tenon-n	a projection on a piece of wood that fits into a slot (= **mortice**) to form a joint
tensile-adj	relating to the degree to which a material can be stretched without breaking
tension-n	a stretching force exerted on a body / emotional stress
tentative-adj	hesitant and uncertain / done with caution to test conditions

tenuous-adj	weak, uncertain, likely to change
	a tenuous excuse / a tenuous grip on reality
tenure-n	the period of time during which someone holds a job or other position
tepid-adj	slightly warm, used of liquids (= **lukewarm**) / lacking enthusiasm
terrace-n	a flat area of land, often cut like steps into a hill for growing crops
terrain-n	the type of ground in a region *hilly terrain*
terse-adj	terse language is brief and curt and shows annoyance
testament-n	a testament to something is proof of its truth or existence
testimonial-n	a formal statement about someone's qualities and abilities
testimony-n	evidence given under oath in a court of law
testy-adj	irritable, peevish, impatient
Teutonic-adj	relating to Germany or to qualities considered to be typically German
therapeutic-adj	relating to the treatment of illness or the improvement of health
thermostat-n	a device used to maintain and regulate temperature
thespian-adj	relating to acting, drama and the theatre (*also* **n**)
thoroughbred-n	a purebred or pedigree animal, esp a horse
thresh-v	to separate grains from the rest of a crop by beating or using a machine
threshold-n	the doorway into a house, or the floor of the doorway
throwback-n	someone or something that is typical of a former time
	The taps are a throwback to Victorian times.
tidings-n-pl	(*dated*) news
tied-adj	a tied pub is required to sell the beer of a particular brewer / a tied cottage is rented only to a current employee
tight-knit-adj	a tight-knit family or community is very close and mutually supportive
tikka-adj	a style of Indian dish where skewered spicy meat is dry-roasted in a clay oven
till-v	(*dated*) to prepare land for planting crops
timbre-n	the quality of a sound, esp of a musical instrument or singing voice
timid-adj	shy, nervous and fearful
tinctorial-adj	relating to the processes of dyeing or colouring processes
tincture-n	a slight or trace amount / a medicine made by mixing a small amount of a drug with alcohol
tinder-n	small pieces of dry wood, used for starting a fire; kindling
tirade-n	a long speech attacking someone or something; a rant

tithe-n	in the past, a tax paid to the church, traditionally a tenth of someone's income
tome-n	a large heavy book on a serious subject
tone-n	**1** the quality of a sound or voice
	2 the firmness and healthy appearance of someone's body, muscles or skin
tonic-n	a medicine aimed at energizing or strengthening you; a pick-me-up
topiary-n	the art of fashioning trees or bushes into recognizable shapes, eg birds or animals
tor-n	a rocky peak of a hill or mountain
toreador-n	a bullfighter, esp one on horseback
torpid-adj	physically or mentally inactive; sluggish, apathetic
torpor-n	the state of lacking energy or enthusiasm
torque-n	the measure of the tendency of a force to rotate an object around an axis
torrid-adj	**1** full of passionate emotions, esp about love and sex
	2 hot and scorching, used of the weather
torsion-n	the rotation or twisting of a body / the state of being twisted
tort-n	an injury or wrong that is liable to compensation via the legal process
totalitarian-adj	relating to a political system in which one political party has total control
tote, the-n	a system of betting money on horse races, the winners receiving a ratio of the total amount bet, minus charges
touchstone-n	a reference point against which something can be compared
tractable-adj	easily managed or controlled
traction-n	**1** the steady pull on a broken bone by weights and pulleys to aid healing
	2 the friction between the wheels of a vehicle and the road to create motion
tranquilizer-n	a drug that makes the recipient calm, sleepy and less anxious
transcendental -adj	beyond the normal range of human experience; mystical
transcribe-v	to write something just as it was said / to copy something from one source to another
transgression-n	a crime or other act that violates a religious or moral rule
transient-adj	temporary, short-lived, fleeting *a transient thought*

transitory-adj	existing for a short time *the transitory life of a mayfly*
transpire-v	to happen, esp of something formerly unknown
trattoria-n	an Italian restaurant, esp one that is simple in style
travail-n	(*literary*) hardship or difficulty
travesty-n	something that is shocking because it is very unfair or unrepresentative *We believe the court hearing is quite illegal and a travesty of justice.*
treachery-n	betrayal
treason-n	the crime of betraying one's country, eg by trying to overthrow its government
treasury-n	**1** the government department responsible for national finance **2** a collection of valuable things / the place where these are kept
treatise-n	a serious book or article about a particular subject
treaty-n	a formal written agreement between two or more countries
trellis-n	an upright latticed wooden support for climbing plants
tremulous-adj	unsteady, quivering, used esp of someone's voice or smile
trenchant-adj	expressed strongly and pointedly *There was trenchant criticism of the company's accounting policies.*
triage-n	the process of prioritization, eg in the accident and emergency department of a hospital, to ensure that the most urgent cases are treated first
tribulation-n	suffering, difficulty, distress
tribunal-n	a law court or committee set up to deal with a particular case or dispute *The case went to an emloyment tribunal.*
tributary-n	a stream or river that flows into a larger river
trigonometry-n	the branch of mathematics dealing with the relationship between angles and the sides of triangles
tripe-n	the stomach lining of a cow or sheep, cooked and eaten as food
trite-adj	dull through overuse; hackneyed, clichéd *The politician's trite language fooled no one.*
troglodyte-n	a cave dweller, esp in prehistoric times / a person regarded as primitive or unsophisticated
troth-n	(*outdated*) a promise / **plight/pledge your troth** to promise to marry someone
troubadour-n	in mediaeval France and Italy, a travelling poet or minstrel
trousseau-n	clothes and possessions collected by a bride before her marriage

truculent-adj	easily annoyed, aggressive
truncate-v	to make something shorter by removing part of it
trunnion-n	in a cannon, one of the cylindrical projections on the side of the barrel that allows vertical rotation
trustee-n	a person legally appointed to look after someone else's money or property
tryst-n	a secret meeting, esp one between lovers; an assignation
tsunami-n	a massive tidal wave caused by undersea seismic activity
tumbleweed-n	a plant growing in dry open areas that breaks from its roots and is blown around by the wind
tumid-adj	**1** swollen or bulging
	2 inflated and pompous, used of language
tundra-n	treeless Arctic or Antarctic regions (*cf* **taiga, steppe**)
tunnel vision-n	**1** the loss or severe reduction of peripheral vision
	2 narrow-mindedness
turbid-adj	muddy or unclear, used esp of water
turbine-n	a machine that uses energy from fluid or gas to turn a wheel and produce power
turbulent-adj	**1** confusing and ever-changing
	Afghanistan's recent turbulent history
	2 full of agitation and violent motion *turbulent waters*
tureen-n	a large, often ornamental, covered dish for serving soup or vegetables at the table
turgid-adj	**1** boring, pompous and complicated
	his turgid, unimaginative and bureaucratic prose style
	2 (*literary*) swollen
turnkey-n	in the past, someone who was in charge of the keys of a prison
turpitude-n	moral depravity, wickedness
turret-n	a small tower on the top of a building, esp a castle
tutelage-n	instruction and guidance provided by a tutor or guardian
tutorial-n	a small discussion class involving a teacher and a small number of students
twine-n	strong string made by twisting several strands together

U

ubiquitous-adj existing or happening everywhere

ulterior-adj hidden; beyond what is evident or assumed *Please know that I have no ulterior motive but only wish to meet you.*

umbrage-n to take umbrage is to feel offended or insulted

unabashed-adj not at all embarrassed or ashamed

unabated-adj continuous, with no reduction in intensity; unstoppable *The war of words between the two countries continues unabated.*

unabridged-adj not shortened or adapted, used esp of a book or speech

unadulterated-adj complete and pure, with nothing added; uncontaminated

unbridled-adj free and unrestrained, used esp of someone's emotions

unctuous-adj charming in an insincere way / greasy or fatty

underling-n an insulting or humorous word for someone who is of lower rank or status than someone else, esp in an organization

underpin-v to support something such as a wall or building by propping it up from below

undulate-v to move or curve gently up and down in a wave-like fashion

unequivocal-adj not ambiguous; clear and definite *There is unequivocal evidence of US involvement.*

unexpurgated -adj full and complete, without the removal of offensive words or images; uncensored

unionist-n someone who supports the joining or remaining together of a political or national entity, esp Northern Ireland remaining part of the UK

Unitarian-n 1 a Christian who rejects the doctrine of the Trinity and believes that God is one being, not three
2 a supporter of centralized government or single-tier local government

unmitigated-adj not reduced in any way; used to emphasize how bad a quality or situation is *an unmitigated disaster for the British economy*

unplugged-adj used to describe a performer using acoustic, not electrical instruments

unrequited-adj not returned or responded to, used esp of love or passion

unseasoned-adj inexperienced / without flavouring such as pepper or herbs

untenable-adj impossible to defend against criticism or attack, used of someone's position in an argument

untoward-adj	unexpected and unfavourable / causing difficulties *an untoward incident*
unwitting-adj	unaware / not done consciously or deliberately *The students have become unwitting victims of inter-departmental politics.*
upbraid-v	to criticize or scold someone severely
uPVC-n-acr	**u**nplasticized **p**oly**v**inyl **c**hloride, a plastic much used in the double-glazing industry
urban-adj	relating to towns and cities rather than the countryside
urbane-adj	pleasant, civilized and socially skilled, used of a person or their behaviour
ursine-adj	relating to bears
usurp-v	to usurp a position, job or title is to seize it from someone without the right to do so
usury-n	(*dated*) the practice of lending money at extreme interest rates
utilitarian-adj	relating to the philosophy that a course of action is morally right if it benefits a majority of people
utopia-n	an imaginary place where everything is perfect
utter-adj	used to emphasize how extremely complete, bad or good something is *a deep shoulder massage is utter bliss*

V

vacillate-v	to keep changing your opinion about something; to waver
vacuous-adj	completely lacking in serious thought / having no sensible meaning
vagaries-n-pl	whimsical or eccentric ideas / unexpected and uncontrollable changes *the vagaries of the weather*
vainglory-n	boastful pride (**adj** = **vainglorious**)
valance-n	a pleated or gathered piece of fabric that hangs from the frame of a bed or shelf / a narrow curtain at the top of a window (= **pelmet**)
vale-n	(*literary*) a valley
valediction-n	a farewell speech, statement or letter
valet-n	a male servant who takes care of his employer's personal needs
valetudinary-adj	relating to persistent ill health, actual or imaginary
valiant-adj	brave and determined, esp in the face of failure or defeat

valour-n	bravery, esp in battle
vamp-n	a manipulative seductress
vanguard-n	1 a military unit that leads the advance into battle
	2 a forward-thinking group with new ideas and concepts
vanity-n	excessive pride in your abilities or appearance; self-conceit
vapid-adj	dull and unimaginative
variegated-adj	with patches or stripes of many colours, used esp of leaves
vascular-adj	relating to the circulatory system of veins and arteries
vassal-n	in feudal times, someone who gave military service to a lord in return for land and protection / a state that is completely dependent on another
vaudeville-n	(*mainly US*) entertainment with comedy, singing and dancing acts, popular in the late 19th and early 20th centuries (= **music hall**)
vehement-adj	expressing strong and passionate feelings or beliefs
venal-adj	dishonest and corrupt; easily bribed
venerable-adj	meriting respect or praise, esp due to great age or wisdom
venial sin-n	in the Roman Catholic church, a small forgivable sin (*cf* **mortal sin**)
veracity-n	truthfulness or honesty / accuracy
verbatim-adv	expressed or written using exactly the same words (*also* **adj**)
verbose-adj	talkative, long-winded, wordy
verdant-adj	(*literary*) green and luxurious, used of grass or pastures
verdigris-n	a green deposit that forms on bronze, brass and copper in damp conditions
verisimilitude-n	the appearance of being true or real
veritable-adj	used before a noun to emphasize the size or extent of something *a veritable feast of movie entertainment*
vermicular-adj	in wavy movements like the tracts of worms / relating to worms
vermin-n	(*usu pl*) animal pests, such as cockroaches and rats
vernacular-n	the commonly spoken dialect of a region, as opposed to the formal written language (*also* **adj**)
vernal-adj	relating to springtime
verve-n	energy, enthusiasm, liveliness
vespers-n	a Christian service held in the evening; evensong
vested-adj	1 having a right to property or to a privilege
	2 **vested interest** = a strong reason for doing something, esp to protect your money, reputation or power

vestigial-adj	remaining but not functioning; rudimentary, used eg of the human appendix / used to describe small remaining amounts of something
viaduct-n	an arched bridge used for carrying a road or railway across a valley
vicarious-adj	experiencing something through another's participation rather than directly *the vicarious thrill of watching your son score a goal*
viceroy-n	the ruler of a region on behalf of a monarch
vicissitudes-n-pl	unexpected changes, esp unpleasant ones, in someone's life or fortunes
vigil-n	a period of time, esp during the night, when people keep watch over a person or situation
vignette-n	a small drawing or portrait at the beginning or end of a book or chapter
vinaigrette-n	a dressing made from oil and vinegar, used on salad
vin de pays-n	French wine given the third highest grade, which guarantees its origin
vin de table-n	inexpensive French wine
virile-adj	strong and active with a high sex drive, used of men
viscera-n-pl	the major organs of the body, esp those in the abdomen
vitiate-v	to invalidate or reduce the effectiveness of something *Reform was vitiated by confusion and a lack of agreed goals.*
vitreous-adj	made of glass / resembling glass
vitriolic-adj	cruel and hateful, used esp of a verbal attack or outburst
vituperation-n	cruel, angry, abusive criticism
vivid-adj	strong and bright in colour / used of a clear and detailed mental image
vivisection-n	the act of performing surgical operations on living animals for the purposes of scientific research
volatile-adj	1 rapidly changing; dangerously uncertain *He warned of even more volatile market conditions in the coming year.*
	2 a volatile substance changes into vapour at a fairly low temperature
volition-n	the power you have to make your own decisions; will
volte-face-n	a sudden and complete reversal of a plan or policy (= **U-turn**)
voracious-adj	1 having a large appetite; ravenous
	2 very eager to get or learn something
votive-adj	presented or dedicated in accordance with a religious vow
vouchsafe-v	(*formal*) to give or grant something to someone

W

wainscot-n	the bottom part of the walls of a room, esp when wood-panelled
wan-adj	pale, tired and unhealthy-looking
wane-v	**1** when the moon wanes, it appears smaller each night (*cf* **wax**)
	2 to gradually become weaker or less important
wanton-adj	**1** unnecessary; without motive *wanton destruction*
	2 (*dated*) used to describe a woman who has sex with a lot of men
Warfarin-n	an anti-coagulant drug used to thin blood and prevent thrombosis
warrant-n	a document authorizing something, eg an arrest by the police
waspish-adj	easily irritated or annoyed
wattle-n	interlocking branches and twigs used as a framework for walls, fences and roofs (**wattle and daub** = this framework covered with a mixture of mud and clay)
wax-v	when the moon waxes, it appears larger each night (*cf* **wane 1**)
wayfarer-n	(*dated*) someone who travels, esp on foot
wean-v	to wean a baby or young animal is to gradually change its diet from milk to solids
weighbridge-n	a machine used for weighing vehicles
wend-v	if you wend your way somewhere, you go there, esp slowly
wet nurse-n	a woman who is paid to breast-feed another woman's baby
wharf-n	the side of the harbour, used for loading or mooring boats
wherewithal-n	the money or means necessary in order to do something. *We no longer have the financial wherewithal to tackle these problems.*
whet-v	to whet a blade is to make it sharper by grinding it on a stone (**whetstone** = the stone used for this)
whim-n	an impulsive idea of the moment
whiplash-n	an injury caused when the neck is suddenly jolted, esp as a result of a traffic accident
whit-n	a very small amount, often used in negatives *Emily did not care one whit that her mother was always away from home.*
whitewash-n	an attempt to hide the unpleasant facts of a situation; a coverup (*also* **v**)
whittle-v	to shape wood into an object using a knife / to reduce in size

wide receiver-n	in American football, a player whose job is to receive long balls from the quarterback
wildcat strike-n	a sudden unofficial strike that does not have trade union support
will o' the wisp-n	1 something elusive, that you cannot reach or attain
	2 an eerie blue glow over marshland caused by the spontaneous combustion of natural gases in rotting organic matter
willy-nilly-adv	1 if something happens willy-nilly, it happens whether you want it to or not *The chairman's agenda will go ahead willy-nilly.*
	2 haphazardly
windfall-n	a sum of money you receive unexpectedly
windlass-n	a mechanical device for lifting heavy things; a winch
winnow-v	to identify and separate the good and bad things or people in a group
winsome-adj	charming, attractive, engaging *a winsome smile*
wistful-adj	yearning for something in a sad way; nostalgic for the past
withers-n-pl	the ridge between the shoulder blades of an animal, esp a horse
woe-n	adversity and misfortune; grief, misery
wont-n	someone's particular habit or custom
work-to-rule-n	a situation where employees work strictly to the rules to reduce output when in dispute with management
wort-n	a sugary mixture of malted grain and water, to be fermented into beer
wraith-n	(*literary*) a ghost or apparition
wrath-n	anger, indignation *He felt the full force of Sarah's wrath.*
wreak-v	to do or cause something bad *Storms wreaked havoc on the roads.*
wrest-v	to wrest something, esp power, from someone is to take it from them by force
wretched-adj	very distressed and sorry-looking
writ-n	a written court order
writhe-v	to wriggle or squirm, esp in pain
wrought-adj	worked and formed into particular shapes *wrought iron gates*
wry-adj	slightly amused and ironic *a wry glance*
wunderkind-n	a young person who is unusually clever or talented (= **child prodigy**)
wuthering-adj	(*literary*) used to describe a strong roaring wind

X

xenophobia-n   a strong dislike and fear of people from other countries and cultures

Y

yakuza-n-pl	in Japan, members of organized criminal gangs
yankee-n	1 an insulting word for an American
	2 a soldier on the Union side in the American civil war
yarn-n	1 thick woollen or cotton thread for knitting or mending
	2 a long story with a lot of interesting detail
yearling-n	a young animal between one and two years old, esp a horse
yeoman-n	in the past, a man who owned the land he farmed / a servant in a royal or noble household
Yiddish-n	a language derived from mediaeval German and elements of Hebrew, spoken by Jews from central and eastern Europe
yoke-n	an oppressive situation that restricts a person's or a country's freedom
	The rural poor are still groaning under the yoke of feudalism.
yokel-n	an insulting word for someone who is uneducated and naïve, esp someone from a rural area
Yom Kippur-n	the annual Jewish Day of Atonement, when Jews pray for forgiveness
yore-n	(*literary*) a period of time in the past, usually long ago

Z

zeal-n   energetic and tireless enthusiasm for a cause

zeitgeist-n   the prevailing spirit of the times; the culture and ideas typical of an era

Zen-n   a Japanese form of Buddhism that focuses on spiritual enlightenment

zenith-n   the highest point reached by the sun or moon during its apparent orbit around a given point of observation / the high point of something *The sun is in its zenith. / The country was at the zenith of its prosperity.*

zephyr-n   a light gentle wind

Zionism-n   the movement that supports the continued development and expansion of the state of Israel

zither-n   a small musical instrument with metal strings, placed horizontally and played using a plectrum